# WHO WAS I?

## CREATING A LIVING HISTORY PERSONA

## A MODEST GUIDE TO THE HOWS AND WHYS

Written and Illustrated by

## Cathy Johnson

*Graphics/Fine Arts Press*

PO BOX 321, EXCELSIOR SPRINGS, MO 64024

Illustration and cover design: Inspired by an original
piece by the Sussel-Washington artist, "His Exelenc
Georg Waschingdon and Ledy Waschingdon" in the
collection of the Abby Aldrich Rockefeller Folk Art
Center; the cover art of this book is by Cathy Johnson.

Typeface: Caslon Antique. The original Caslon face was
designed by Wm. Caslon (1692-1766), who was the first
of a famous line of type designers and founders. Caslon
began his working life as an apprentice to a London
engraver of gun locks and barrels, then opened his own
shop to begin making bookbinder's stamps and silver
chasing. He founded his first type foundry in 1720 with
a loan from printers John Watts and Wm. Bowyer.

Library of Congress Cataloging-in-Publication Data
Johnson, Cathy (Cathy A.)
        Who Was I; Creating a Living History Persona
1st edition
        ISBN 0-9638158-1-4
        1. History--2. Living History..3. Research
Manufactured in the United States of America

# Table of Contents

# Acknowledgments:

No book—even a small one like this--happens without a great deal of help in the form of proofreading, fact-checking, advice, and, of course, encouragement. I owe a debt of gratitude to many people; if I have left someone out, I offer my sincere apologies. Thanks go to Heritage Books for kind permission to quote extensively from *The Settlement and Indian Wars of the Western Parts of Virginia and Pennsylvania, 1763-1783*, by the Rev. Joseph Doddridge. Individuals who come to mind are Steve Wilson, interpreter, professional (and inveterate) researcher; Peter and Debra Goebel, Goose Bay Workshops; Dave Hinkley of Historical Markers, Ltd.; Saundra Ros Altman, Past Patterns; Mark Baker, historian, fine writer and master of persona; Beth Gilgun; Ted and Christine Carr Reese of the Female Spectator Revived; Linda Marin and Brian Bradley, Bradley Company of the Fox; Stacy Roth, author of *Past into Present* (U. of N. Carolina Press); Jay Anderson, Professor of History at Utah State University and author of *Time Machines, The Living History Reader*, etc. (American Association for State and Local History); Donlyn Myers, Smoke & Fire News; Ed and C. J. Wilde, Wilde Weavery and Trading Co.; Bill Scurlock, editor, *Muzzleloader Magazine*; Kathleen and Fritz Kannik, Kannik's Korner; Barbara and Denny Duffy, period musicians; F.L. Watkins, Folump Enterprises; John Curry, contributing editor of *On the Trail*; Mary Ellen Rowe, Ph.D., Assistant Professor of History at Central Missouri State University; fellow reenactors Duke Drury and Bishop David Jones; and my husband Harris, who endures my obsession with unfailing good humor and support.

*Harris P.*

# Introduction:

This little book is a humble offering in a growing field. It is intended to help the beginner along the road to finding a living history persona and to assist the longtime reenactor or interpreter by offering previously underutilized sources of information. Herein also are suggestions for avoiding some common mistakes along with a list of appropriate demonstrations.

The basic techniques involved in creating a living history persona are the same for all eras and all places; the sources of research included here should be useful to anyone with an interest in the field. Many periods are being interpreted today, from the Pilgrims at Plimoth Plantation to the Victorian and Edwardian eras and beyond. My own experience and interests have taken me deeper into the region of the Illinois/Louisiana/Missouri Territory and its history. Much has been written already about the Eastern colonies. This book brings to light sources from many different areas of the country,

Much has been written already about the Eastern colonies. This book brings to light sources from many different areas of the country, including a huge stretch of landscape from the Appalachians to the Plains, from the Great Lakes to the Gulf of Mexico.

The European-influenced history of this territory goes back much earlier than many people imagine. From the earliest French exploration of the Missouri, Kaw, and Mississippi River basins to the influx of British, German, Scots-Irish, and American naturalists and explorers, longhunters and settlers into Kentucky, Tennessee, Missouri, Arkansas, and beyond, the timeline stretches from the 1600s to the present day. Factoring in the early non-European inhabitants puts occupation back to Ice Age and earlier. For my own use, zeroing in on this specific area allows me to burrow much deeper into the past--and to feel at home there.

As with any offering of this sort, there will be differences of opinion or interpretation. Should we mention only what was the most common or include some of the unusual in the interests of presenting a more complete picture? Many writers choose the former, believing the common is the safest choice, and they are right. It is. But it is my decision to do the latter, presenting a bit of the other side of the picture to make sure it is balanced. Besides, "common" doesn't mean uniform; those legions of ordinary folk were not cookie-cutter replicas of one another. Then as now, human beings had brains and used them; had separate identities, ethnic backgrounds, economic and educational levels, job opportunities, luck, skills, and interests. This book reflects that basic fact of humanity--our wonderful diversity. Human nature, at least, doesn't change.

Of course, governmental, religious, and societal mores and customs prevailed, whatever your chosen time period. The majority of women were housewives or expected to marry. Most men worked for a living, and at fairly routine activities. But within those boundaries were a wide range of occupations, activities and supplemental sources of income for both genders. Talents, then as now, were varied, as were individual tastes.

Some people lived and died by fashion; others didn't give a rap. Slaves, indentured servants and occupants of the backwoods were probably not concerned with such things, sometimes to the consternation of the more educated travelers who wrote down their observations (see Woodmason and Schoolcraft). Nonconformists and just plain eccentrics had other things on their minds--the descriptions of unusual and sometimes bizarre clothing worn by the naturalists Audubon and Constantine Rafinesque, hermits (Doddridge 76), and travelers like Estwick Evans in his tight-fitting buffalo-hair coveralls (*Early Western Travels*, Thwaites) are cases in point.

Some (regardless of gender) were educated, some were not, and some were only slightly literate. Some were upstanding citizens; others were rakes and bawds.

Rigid stereotypes don't offer a fair picture of the reality of the human experience; they also lead to stagnation and boredom in our own life as interpreters. We present an incomplete picture if we say women never worked outside the home. We muddy the issue if we suggest all men were experienced with firearms, say, or that they all hunted for a living--or even as a supplement (Schoolcraft 70). We perpetuate a misconception if we give the impression that most people were largely self-sufficient, manufacturing everything themselves. Some did, some did not (depending partly on circumstance and locale), and those that did lived at once on a much simpler and much more difficult (and time-consuming) subsistence level than those who did not. Barter has always been a part of our experience, and those who were accomplished in one area traded goods or services with those with needed offerings. A surprising variety of items were available, even on the frontier--research is the key. In the towns and cities of the late 1700s and early 1800s, many types of fabrics and foodstuffs were available. Imports included fruit preserved in brandy, sausages, anchovies, great quantities of olive oil, and vermicelli and other pastas, which were moved over "hundreds of leagues and vast wildernesses" (C. C. Robin 44). That is not to say "If they'da had it, they'da used it," just that proper investigation can broaden your interpretation in interesting and historically accurate ways.

Frontier life was difficult but varied. Backwoods families in Illinois, Kentucky, Maine, Carolina, Louisiana and Missouri Territory (whites and Americans as well as French and even some Indians) dressed in linen, linsey-woolsey, wool, some cotton, and buckskin as well as some satins, silks and other fabrics, according to primary documents (Kalm, Schoolcraft, de Finiels, Henry Marie Brackenridge, Pitot, Belting, *et al.*) They subsisted on game and wild foods in addition to simple gardens often consisting only of corn and beans, and traded for the rest. There was play as well as work.

The dilemma of whether to reflect this diversity in discussing clothing or to stick with the common, more uniform styles (which are considerably less controversial) was a tough one. Some of the clothing in this book is admittedly somewhat unusual; I hope I have mentioned that, either in the text or on the art. Everything that was drawn came from original primary sources such as paintings and illustrations or from original garments. For instance, I have seen examples of at least six chemises or shifts with ruffles at the bottom, including those in *Revolution in Fashion* (Kyoto Fashion Institute 36) and *Eighteenth Century Clothing at Williamsburg* (Baumgarten 17) or depicted by William Hogarth (Quennel 97).

Styles overlapped, of course. Everyone didn't wake up one day to discover the fashion had changed and burn their old clothes. For instance, it's impossible to say that fly-front breeches had disappeared by the 1760s or even 1770s, to be immediately supplanted by fall-front breeches, which came in circa 1750 (Waugh, *The Cut of Men's Clothes*, 55). Some men undoubtedly held onto clothing if it had wear left in it, or simply clung to styles they liked. Breeches themselves lasted well into the 19th century, especially as court, country, or sport clothes, and among the unfashionable (Ibid. 116). They are still worn as formal livery. Garment names changed as well; what was called breeches may also have been known as culottes (French). Trousers were also trowsers, trews, pants, pantaloons (which were also a different garment more closely resembling footless tights), or *sans culottes*, which were worn in protest to the gentry's more formal breeches in the French Revolution. Chemises were also known as shimmies, shifts, and smocks.

Practical work clothes, especially, changed slowly. The unfitted jacket-like garments we call shortgowns were worn for a period of more than 100 years. What our forebears called them is unclear, though a few documents do refer to "short gowns." Some had small gussets at the bottom, when they were made from narrow widths of fabric; other original garments show no such gusset. Some had long sleeves, some much shorter. Some shortgowns were pinned to hold them closed, some were tied; a few buttoned. Some had high waists during the Regency period. (See "Short Gowns" by Claudia Kidwell, in the journal *Dress*, Vol. 4, 1978, pp. 30-65.) At least one shortgown in the collection of Cherry Hill, in Albany, New York, was probably intended for dressier wear; it was finely crafted and decorated with ruffles on the ends of its long sleeves.

Bedgowns continued over a long period as well (mentioned by the Rev. Doddridge in 1763, shown by Garsault in 1769, still in use at least by the mid-19th century as seen in period art), especially among older women. As ever, the young were in the market for the new and daring, the calculated-to-attract-the-opposite-sex, as de Finiels, Woodmason, and Doddridge point out. Seeing a mix of clothing eras and styles--within reason--probably comes closest to reflecting what you might have seen in a normal community of your chosen period. "Within reason" is, of course, the operative phrase. That's why it pays to know what was common and to make your deviations from the norm logical, practical, *and documentable*.

But despite this apparent emphasis on clothing, the most visible clue to persona, we should remember that what people did and thought, believed and fought for (or against) were *always* more important than what they wore. Your persona is much more than your period attire. What you do, what you say, and what you think gives a far clearer picture of history.

# ꙮWho Was I?ꙮ

## Creating a Living History Persona

Not everyone who is interested in living history wants to create a persona, a specific individual to base your interpretation on--especially when just starting out. Many people choose a more generalized interpretation--a goodwife of the American Revolution, a middle-ground longhunter, an 1812 soldier. The primary reason for developing a persona--someone, in effect, to *be* as you are involved in living history reenacting or interpretation--is simply that it lets you focus. It's always easier to relate to the particular than to the universal. It's also easier to get inside of something with texture and depth that is capable of piquing your curiosity and capturing your imagination than a one-dimensional generalization. Your search for the bits and pieces of history--period trivia--becomes much more particular, much more specific. So does your interpretation.

But the real truth, for most of us, is that having a persona is an opportunity to *play*, no matter how serious about it we may be. We all loved to dress up and pretend to be someone else when we were young; why should it be frightening or daunting now? In fact it's as much fun as ever. Sharing the facts of history with others is important, of course; I don't mean to put down that good work. We can't afford to lose track of the past that brought us where we are today. There is often serious motivation for all this fun--but that's no reason why we shouldn't enjoy it to the full. Whether you make your living as an interpreter at a historic site or do it strictly for enjoyment, getting specific--creating your own persona--makes it *real*; the illusion, for you and for the public, is complete.

Consider our middle-ground longhunter. Maybe he came from Ireland by way of Pennsylvania; his name is Patrick Kerry. His father is a peat-cutter, his mother a midwife. The family has always been poor. Patrick managed passage to this country--with the encouragement of his older brother Brian--by indenturing himself to a Philadelphia carpenter who treated him well enough but unfailingly condescended to him. Patrick had originally planned to settle near the coast, but it was too much like the old country--he's already worked out his indenture and doesn't plan to answer to much of anybody, ever again--the freedom, opportunity, and adventure of the frontier suits him.

He was in love once, back in County Mayo, but she wed another; he's unmarried, but interested. He likes music, plays fiddle and has a fine tenor voice which you may never hear--he's painfully shy. He's good with his hands, as a carpenter must be, and built his small cabin and its furnishings. He's still looking for Brian, who seems to have disappeared since his last letter.

And how is it with that anonymous goodwife? She's the daughter of a newspaper publisher, one of the first in the growing town of New York. Father and Mother are loyal to the Crown, but Abigail Hatfield is quite acclimated to the New World, where she was born. She is literate, and keeps a journal; she corresponds with Ann Franklin, who became the first female editor of an American newspaper in 1762, the Newport Rhode Island Mercury. She considers herself a patriot, as is her husband. This creates tension in her family. As Loyalists, her parents haven't spoken to her since the beginning of the war, and the break pains her deeply.

She learned to use herbs for healing and for dyestuffs from

2

her mother; she's read of their use by the Indians who first occupied this land as well. She married young and has already lost two children, but the others are well and strong and look to be taking after their father, who is serving with the American forces. She is very proud of the young ones, but worried now that it is necessary to care for them and the family business while her husband is away; sometimes the fighting gets too close, and there has been an outbreak of cholera that her herbs do little to dispel. She takes snuff and has become a crack shot out of necessity; sometimes food is scarce. Truth to tell, she enjoys shooting her own double-trigger rifle and knows how to formulate gunpowder.

See what I mean? Now you know these people. Patrick is a human being. You can begin to judge what his reactions might be, what his skills are, what he knows, what his beliefs and politics might be. Abigail takes on dimension and substance. You get an idea how she might dress, what she might do of an evening, and you know she could use that flintlock to protect her children if need be. She's not a shadowy figure any more, but someone you can relate to.

Some organizations actually require you to develop a persona if you become a member; others simply encourage it. The NWTA (North West Territory Alliance) and BAR (Brigade of the American Revolution) strongly suggest such a persona; when you join the Coalition of Historical Trekkers you are asked to submit a brief description of your persona. The Living History Foundation in Chantilly, Virginia, offers an excellent guideline to creating or discovering your alter ego. The value of doing so has been recognized by individuals, organizations and museums for many years; it's a great way to bring history to life, animating the sometimes sterile environment of a traditional museum. (Imagine Colonial Williamsburg or Plimoth Plantation without interpreters and you begin to get the picture.)

Don't let the idea of developing such a character make you nervous. A persona isn't intended to ask more of you than you're willing to give, and it certainly isn't meant to take the fun out of

3

living history interpretation. Instead, having a persona enhances your enjoyment. We now have a key to the time machine, that magic conveyance most of us involved in living history search for so diligently. Once aboard, we can forget about 20th Century concerns and complications and try on a whole new set--or rather, an *old* set. Life wasn't actually simpler, just different--different problems, challenges, expectations and even codes of behavior. It's the *differences* that transport us to another time. Having a persona is like having a guide to the past, one who is both intriguing and intimate.

Besides focus (*and* fun), there are several other reasons for developing a persona. It can be a way to use your existing skills or knowledge, a natural outgrowth of your present-day interests "backdated" to the period you choose. A friend who is a proficient leather worker often portrays a leather worker of the 18th or early 19th century. Another who makes his day-to-day living as a coppersmith chooses that as his period persona as well. I am a naturalist by trade in present time, with a working knowledge of useful plants, wild animals and their tracks, and a bit of geology. On a tour of the woods with flintlock in hand, those things still interest me. I can't pretend they don't, and I can't ignore them. So my persona is also a naturalist--or a backwoods woman who knows herbs, a woman like those mentioned in Schoolcraft, Doddridge, Kalm, and McKnight.

Often, a persona develops out of a specific skill, which can grow from the environment you use it in. In other words, say you are intrigued by a specific fort which portrays a specific time frame; you decide to volunteer. There are demonstrations or jobs that may be especially appropriate there, perhaps ones that make use of skills you already possess. As you work, you begin to think about the kind of person who might have done these things 200 years ago give or take-- where he came from, what her economic level is, why they'd be here in the first place. Before you know it, a persona is born.

If you're fortunate enough to have a military roster or list of civilian personnel attached to that particular fort, you can choose to interpret one of those people.

It may be best--and certainly easier--to interpret a more ordinary person rather than a hero, a villain or a flamboyant character. After all, there are more of us "normal" types around today. We can relate to the everydayness of these earlier Americans. When you stay in the context of your resource and think about what you're doing and why you're doing it, interpreting becomes much simpler and more natural. It isn't necessary to memorize an unwieldy set of facts to spiel off by rote; you're inside the character and acting from the context of the situation. John Curry, who writes for *Smoke & Fire News* and *On the Trail*, publications devoted to living history, says that when he and his trekking friends are in the woods in their personas, they don't change their names; they are themselves--but in the 18th century.

On the other hand, if you choose to interpret someone with *unusual* interests, occupations, or talents, creating a persona helps you be more confident in your portrayal. It gives you an avenue of research. It helps you to find answers to questions--your own as well as those of visitors or other reenactors. If you find someone who *actually did* the unusual things that strike fire in your imagination, you can discover why they did what they did, what were the factors that led up to or hindered that pursuit. You can learn what was involved *then* in contrast or complement to what is involved in a similar occupation *now*. Period books may help, as do state and local historical societies, museums and living history sites.

Choosing to portray the more common or generic person is fine when you're starting out; it is easier and less of a challenge. But as you learn more, your interpretation will develop from the Everyman (or woman) to the specific, to the human. And humans are as individual as their fingerprints; always have been, when you get beneath the surface.

Ethnic origins are useful in helping you formulate a persona-- choose your own or a culture that has always fascinated you. Ethnicity can provide a range of types or personas to choose from that will make your portrayal more accurate and certainly more interesting. Not everyone dressed, talked, or thought alike, and sometimes those differences were due to the country of their birth. At Missouri's Fort Osage, surviving duty rosters give the nationality of many of the soldiers. By extrapolation we may assume their wives were similarly diverse, as may have been the other civilians attached to the fort. Remember that different ethnic groups may have dressed differently. French and Germans, among others, wore wooden shoes; French women in this area were often described as wearing a scarf knotted over the forehead rather than a cap or hat. Scots or Irish women were particularly fond of shawls. Immigrants often clung to items of clothing or other style preferences brought with them from Europe which made them feel more at home in their new environment. Genealogical research can help you discover your own background; it can be illuminating as well as fun, shedding light on an entire culture. There are books written especially for the novice, outlining the best and easiest ways to research and where to find the information you're after. Check with your local library.

Language and dialect can contribute to your persona. If you know French, Spanish, Gaelic, German, Dutch or Russian and it's appropriate to your persona, foreign language gives a flavor of our young republic--which was, after all, made up of immigrants. If you know only a few words, that can be effective, too. Dialect--English with an Irish lilt, say, really sets the mood, but be careful. Listen to a good movie dialect or even foreign language tape. Obviously, Gaelic does not sound like Liverpool British.

Pay attention to your *English*, too. Look up definitions of words and phrases in a period dictionary and salt your conversation with appropriate terms. Some are hilarious (Try *A Classical Dictionary of the Vulgar Tongue* or *Colonial American English*--see Bibliography.) Have a "cat lap" or "scandal broth" (tea); expect a "crow fair" (gathering of clergy.) Be aware that some words may not yet exist, i.e., "telephone," "grunge," and even "hello" ("halloo" was the common earlier form). Other words have changed

6

substantially (i.e., "cool," "neat," "buff"); try to avoid them or replace them with appropriate terminology. *The Oxford English Dictionary* is a great help here; your library should have the multi-volume set.

Religion, too, may play a role in forming your persona. Are you a French or Irish Catholic, a Quaker, a Russian Orthodox, a Native American, a pagan? Each of these colors your interpretation and adds depth and dimension, another layer to explore. It's not that you need to portray clergy or share your religion with all and sundry, just be aware how it might affect your persona.

In a recent telephone interview, Jay Anderson, author of *Time Machines: the World of Living History* and *The Living History Sourcebook*, suggested a useful technique for getting to know this past self: "Consider your present age. Then, look at the period you are interpreting—say 1812—and subtract to find the year you were 'born.' Perhaps that puts you back to 1763; you would have remembered the Revolutionary War, perhaps lost a father or older brother. At the least you would have heard stories from the old veterans.

"What would have affected your life? What medical and scientific advances would you have seen? What new technologies? What advantages and disadvantages did the aftermath of independence cause your family? Who is now President of this new Republic—and who would like to be? Going a bit deeper, ask yourself what you would have known or remembered at age 10, or 20, or 30. This is most fun to do in a group of like-minded people who can share their 'experiences' and introduce topics you might not have thought of. Many people can act as mentors in a situation like this, and it's a wonderful way to break the ice," says Anderson.

# ꙮ Take It Easy ꙮ

**E**ven if you do create such a role model for yourself, that doesn't mean you're locked into first-person interpretation, which some people find a little unnerving. (In first person you might say "I'm first mate on this whaler, and you'd be hard put to find another who'd seen what I have"; in third person you'd be more likely to say "Abraham Foster was first mate on this whaler and visited many ports of call.") It's like being an actor with entirely ad-libbed lines--exhilarating but a bit of a roller-coaster.

Even if you interpret history in *third* person, your real or fictional persona can still be a help to you, whether or not you choose to portray him or her directly. (In fact, unless you just want to share your persona, no one else even need know it exists.) What you say or do will have a truer ring if you understand the personal dimension. This research into character development offers a doorway into the period on a different, more individual level, and allows you to understand history in a way not possible before. Your persona can also act as a general guideline to attire or accoutrements and what would be appropriate to your character and his or her time frame.

If you choose a real person to base your interpretation on, it's like a treasure hunt as you dig up all the facts you can find. Sometimes, if your subject is famous or has kept a personal journal, that's relatively easy. If not, then flesh out your characterization with what facts you can find about the real person, then expand your interpretation with logical suppositions based on the lives of similar individuals. A fictional but representative person you concoct yourself may be more satisfying--and it's certainly easier than trying to "be" someone who actually existed. You can portray a fictional friend or relative of a real person, instead.

My original persona, who still appears from time to time, was a Quaker who had been put out of her meeting for an inordinate love of music and other "worldly" things. I chose a Quaker because these people educated their daughters as well as their sons, with an emphasis on the sciences. Since I'm a naturalist and artist in "real life," my interests tend to run along these lines; I can research backwards to discover what was known or believed about the natural world at the time. As my base I can use Jane Colden, the colonial naturalist who was known by Ben Franklin, John and William Bartram and probably Peter Kalm, who mentions meeting her family. (Kalm 216, 257, 299, 356, *et al*) Bits of information as to attitude, knowledge, and methods of working could be incorporated from naturalists of the opposite sex, as well, since so much more is known about Audubon, John Bradbury, Peter Kalm and others.

More often, now, I am simply a backwoods woman who has learned the useful plants and understands hunting, gathering, and the basics of gardening to supplement a subsistence way of life--closer to what I enjoy doing on a tour of the woods. She can read some, and sketches a bit, but she is not so fancy as the proper Quaker lady. Good old "Kate Kelly" is a composite based on descriptions of self-sufficient women in the Louisiana/Missouri Territory as well as on some interesting ladies from Virginia, Ohio, and Maine, and taken from descriptions in primary documents such as Henry Rowe Schoolcraft and Nicolas de Finiels, among others. Personas change with time, as you learn more or find a better fit with your interests and personality. Kate, the woodsrunner, fits.

## ⚜Before You Begin⚜

Do a bit of digging before formulating your persona; this will not only save time but expense; after all, there's no need to outfit yourself with a $300 British officer's justaucorps if you're a common sailor. Get an idea of what would and would not have been done or known in your chosen time or place. Keep an eye out for interesting types, representative (or unusual) people who would make good subjects. Check books that offer an overview of a time or place; do you like the political atmosphere, the clothing, the possibilities for action or learning or demonstrations? Does one era speak to you more than another? You may love Revolutionary War period to the virtual exclusion of all else; you may prefer the Renaissance or the Civil War; you may respond to the French and Indian War, Westward Expansion or the Santa Fe Trail era. A bit of preliminary research can help you set off in the right direction--for *you*.

# ꙮCLOTHES DON'T MAKE THE MANꙮ
## But They Do Help Shape Your Interpretation

Although hardly the most important aspect of your persona, clothing *is* the most obvious manifestation. It's what you choose to outwardly express your personality, occupation or station; it's what the public sees first. If there are glaring mistakes or anomalies here, it may throw doubt on the rest of your interpretation.

If you wear something uncommon, be prepared to document your choice. You may want to use the rule of thumb of the "magic threes" here as writer/historian Mark Baker suggests: "Can you find an unusual item or practice in three separate sources? If so, it did indeed exist as written in the first primary source" (Baker, note to author, 10 June 1995). You are in a much better position to document your choice. This is a good way to check if a certain type of firearm was available in your time period, or an unusual style of chemise or waistcoat was worn. Written descriptions generally tend to be more difficult to visualize; a drawing, sketch or illustration from the time period can be very valuable. Just take into consideration the skill (or lack of it) of the artist, and what he or she was trying to portray (some were going for Biblical or classical scenes, either with appropriate clothing or clothing of their time period superimposed on the historical scene). Consider whether the painting was a formal

10

portrait, which was more likely to be stylized, or a genre painting or landscape with people in it. Also worth considering is whether the painting was copied from another source, and whether the illustration was done at the time or decades later.

Look at period paintings and engravings, but keep in mind the time frame, locale, occupation and income of the subject. If your persona is a Southwestern trader, you'll look odd dressed like one of Rogers' Rangers; if you want to portray a Colonial New England goodwife, you probably wouldn't wear that Colonial *French*-style turban, no matter how much you liked the look. This is especially true if you are at an event or a place that has a specific time frame.

What you *don't* want to do is zero in on something "cool" and insist on wearing that to all events in all time frames, whether or not it is appropriate or fits your persona. Not everybody should look like Hawkeye--or Scarlett.

A friend tells me that when his group goes to an event at a specific site to interpret a specific activity, they meet beforehand to go over what each of them is wearing or carrying. They critique each one in turn, and if something doesn't fit in they ditch it before the event opens. Whereas you might not have that kind of opportunity, it is a good practice to critique *yourself*. Ask "Is what I have on consistent with the specified time and place this event's activities?" If you've done a bit of homework, the answer will probably be yes.

## ✤FIRST TIME OUT✤

Nobody wants to feel like a newcomer, even if you are. We are all nervous about our first outing in these funny new clothes-- though you can be sure it won't be long until they feel perfectly normal. If a site asks you to submit photos of yourself in period attire or clothing (usually called some variation on that theme rather than "costume"[1]), do it; don't be intimidated. It's a good opportunity to polish your outfit. Even better, take your gear (or yourself *in* your gear) to a veteran reenactor, brigade leader or researcher, or site administrator. Ask if what you have is all right, then cross-check--do your homework. Look at period, primary sources for yourself. Don't believe it when *anyone* says to you "gentlemen *always* . . ." or "ladies *never* . . . " Fill in the blanks with whatever; I've heard a dozen variations on this theme, and what is true, I promise you, is that *always* and *never* don't apply to human beings--or to establishing an argument. What is practical is to consider those things that were most likely; what was generally or commonly done. But then as now, we were individuals--again, with individual backgrounds, ethnic influences, economic levels, activities, availability of goods and degrees of skill--and differing tastes as well.

Consider the ongoing argument concerning ladies' headgear. It has been said that women "always" wore a cap; some sites insist upon it. What the primary documents and contemporary illustrations reveal is quite the contrary, however. The Rev. Charles Woodmason describes the hair of his female Carolina parishioners: "tying it up behind in a Bunch like the Indians--being hardly one degree removed from them . . . " (Woodmason 61.) Nicolas de Finiels describes the young Creole women of the Louisiana Territory: "Long tresses of hair are no longer restrained with cotton kerchiefs; they float in voluptuous swirls or are artfully braided. Ribbons and flowers are skillfully added in order to draw out more advantageously, *divers nuances* (de Finiels 115). Lady Jane Cole wrote in 1754 that "People who have covered their heads for fifty years now leave off caps and think it becomes them, in short we try to out-do our patterns, the

---

[1] "Costume" is for the stage or movie set; it may look right, but it is not necessary correctly constructed, of the proper fabric, or even comfortable to wear.

French in every ridiculous vanity."[2] (This seems to confirm that it was not only wenches or backwoods women who shunned caps.)

Lady in riding habit with gun and falcon — after Watteau (1684–1721) (pencil sketch)

turbaned Creole after Anna Maria von Phul, 1818

after "Mrs John Montresor", John Singleton Copley
c.1776

after Lewis Miller c.1849

Kneeling — after J. Baptiste Pater early 18th c.

after "Anne Izard", Gilbert Stuart
c.1794

after "Deborah Richmond," artist unknown, 1791

straw hat after C.W.E. Dietrich. pearls
c.1750

after Anna Maria von Phul, 1818

after Martha Custis (Washington) Wollaston
c.1757

after Henrietta Dering Johnston. 1715

after "Fitting" from "Le Corset,"
c.1780

after W.A. Pyne

after "Women with Long Blonde Hair" (and bangs), Wm. Jennys, c.1806

"Mrs Yeaman vaulting"

horseback circus woman after "Birth Certificate for Joseph Scott Fritz," attrib. to Henry Young c.1821

after "Miss Rebecca Freese" (artist unknown), c.1835–1840

blends into background

after "The Apple Gatherers," artist unknown, c.1820

after "Sarah Prince" by John Brewster Jr. c.1801

[2] Lady's Jane's letter is quoted in Waugh, *Cut of Women's Clothes. 1600-1930*, p 116

The sketches included here were all taken from original sources; there are women from all different economic levels, ethnic backgrounds, locales. The original artworks were done for a variety of reasons, from commissioned portraits to illustrations to birth certificates and rough sketches. I stopped drawing only because I ran out of room on the page; there are dozens of others.

Whereas it may be true to say that women *generally* wore day caps, there is abundant documentation, both written and in the form of period sketches, engravings and paintings, to convincingly argue the case that a number did not, certainly not at all times and in all places. They may have worn nothing at all, or a tam or straw hat without a cap, as at left. (At times, "head covering" meant a simple ribbon or flower.) Check, especially, genre and folk paintings; the 18th C. portraits by Henrietta Johnston, the first professional artist in this country, C. 1703; the prolific John Singleton Copley; Gilbert Stuart; C.W.E. Dietrich, C. 1750; Jean Baptiste Pater ("Les Baigneuses" at Kansas City's Nelson Gallery); a particularly interesting portrait of Martha Washington in the NY Historical Society; and a few of W.H. Pyne's engravings, especially of the troop of entertainers. One looks like Medusa!

The most compelling reason for wearing a cap for most 20th-century reenactors is to cover inappropriate modern hairstyles. If your hair is short, very permed, or bobbed, it does need covering--unless you do Regency period. (Again, "always" doesn't apply.)

Gentlemen "always wore their waistcoats"--until they took them off to work the garden, go hunting, cut the wood, dip sheep, or dance a jig. (See the paintings of Benjamin Henry Latrobe and W. H. Pyne's engravings.) C.C. Robin noted in 1803 how ridiculous men looked dressed in formal woolens in the heat of Colonial Louisiana. When he asked who these men were, he was told "they were the gentry . . . and voluntary slaves to our fashions . . . which formed a cult of imitation as painful as it was slavish . . . " (Robin 47). And of course, not everyone is a gentleman--or a lady.

There are some things that give the newcomer away; we've all been there. It's as though there is a progression of steps everyone passes through. For the most part these missteps are easy to avoid; you'll save both time and money.

1. When *everything* looks brand new and too clean, you stand out. Get a little wear on your clothing. Some backwoods reenactors don't wash their things for months at a time, if at all; they look right (and probably smell that way, too), but you needn't go quite that far if you don't want to. Some stains or a natural dyebath will do wonders for too-new outfits. Wrinkles help. Sun fading of work clothes is natural. Neatly-mended rips look right (clothing was often expensive or time consuming to produce, and people took care of it if possible.) *Rips* are good, for a time. Not everything needs to look worn, of course; people replaced articles of clothing as they wore out--and as they could. Mending was constant. But a broken-in piece or two adds authenticity. Re-cutting a garment to alter it to fit a later fashion was very common.

Artificially aging some of your gear is fine, if necessary. Even better is to *wear* your period attire. Work in it. Cook in it. Eat in it. Volunteer at your favorite site and soon your outfit will have aged authentically on its own.

after "The Laundress" by Chardin

Soap was available, of course, including olive oil-based castile; lye soap was made at home, but laundry days in winter might be few and far between. Some fabrics could not be washed, and clothing was brushed, aired, or "freshened" with vodka to clean it.

2.  Look for natural fabrics and materials. Linen, wool (not reprocessed or recycled wool), linsey-woolsey (wool and linen woven together), fustian (cotton and linen), silk, and even cotton--now common but once expensive and perhaps difficult to come by (or banned by law)--and leathers; these are your best choices. They look and feel right; they drape correctly. Polyester looks like polyester-- too neat and wrinkle-free.

Be aware that fabrics that are now available may have the same names as those two hundred years ago, but they may otherwise be quite different. Osnaburg was linen, not oatmealy cotton; muslin was a fine, light cotton, not the low end of the yard goods line it is now. Interestingly, "cotton" sometimes referred to wool fabric, from the 15th century onward, perhaps because raising the nap created a cottony appearance (Montgomery 206). Homespun cottons have a nice handmade look--but most are probably not spun in anybody's home. Not that today's homespuns, osnaburgs and muslins aren't viable choices, in some cases; they're just not the *same* choices. Many fabrics that were available in the 18th and 19th centuries can no longer be found, but others, like jean, dimity, and nankeen, are available if you look around. Check bibliography for sources.

3.  If you choose to dye your fabrics, use natural dyes--walnut husks, acorns or oak bark, goldenrod, sumac, onion skins, Osage orange, or the more rare (and expensive) indigo, logwood, and cochineal, for instance. Osnaburg does have the look of homespun; if you dye it, it's less obviously recognizable as the modern fabric it is. Be aware that dyeing cotton or linen takes longer than you might think. These plant-based fibers are much more difficult to dye than silk or wool. A cold walnut dyebath may take several days (or weeks) to reach the degree of color you want. It is one of the easier dyes, but it does take longer than the commercial product. Natural dyeing is an art; different mordants are used to pretreat fabric or are added during the dye process to help the fibers take the color. There are a number of good books on the market; check your library.

4. If you're making your own clothes, try to use hand-sewing where it shows (or for the whole garment.) Even if you're a beginner and your stitches are wobbly as hen tracks, remember there were home sewers of varying degrees of skill then, too. See Kathleen Kannik's *The Lady's Guide to Plain Sewing* for period techniques and good, clear, well-illustrated instruction (see Bibliography). Use thread of natural fiber, too. If you dye your clothing later, polyester thread won't take dye the same way your fabric will--it won't match. Quilting thread, which is all cotton, is a good choice.

5. Tiny, multicolored calico prints are great for quilters, but probably not for reenactors until the mid-19th Century at least. Solids, stripes, plaids or checks are much more representative. 18th Century calicos (named after Calicut, their city of origin in India) were first plain, then much larger prints, often hand-colored and expensive. They may even have been linen (Pitot 178). They were described as "plain, printed, stained, dyed, chintz, muslin and the like . . . The printing of calicoes was first set on foot in London about 1676, and has long been a most important article of commerce."[3] By the early 19th century, technology had caught up with demand, and fabrics were roller-printed. Patterns were small, somewhat geometric, and drab in color at that time.

6. Buckskin (or elkskin, or whatever) wasn't brightly colored, as much commercially available leather is today. If that's what you've bought, you'll want to dull it down. Some Native American ceremonial clothing was white, but in general white leathers worn for everyday mark you as a newcomer. Soaking them in a strong walnut or tannic acid bath will make overly white or yellow leather look more natural. (Many sutlers carry tannic acid.)

---

[3] From Thomas Sheraton's Encyclopedia, 1804-1807.

Daniel Morgan, after an engraving of a sketch by John Trumbull c. 1781

Hunting Frock

And incidentally, heavily fringed leathers are more appropriate to the 1960s than the 1760s. Fringe was often used, of course; many period drawings show hunting frocks of linen, cotton or leather with fringed collars, capes, sleeves, etc., such as this one of Daniel Morgan. But the Western movie look is generally not appropriate.

7. Shoes *are* difficult when starting out, but hippie mocs or fleece-lined moccasin-style bedroom slippers don't get it, nor do most of the *slick* mocs you see advertised. Original Mohegan and Penobscot moccasins are similar to loafer-style slippers, however (Hatt 169). Until you're sure of your chosen period and are ready to buy a pair of admittedly expensive reproductions, try to find black or natural colored shoes with leather soles or get a pair of simple *authentic* moccasins. (Make your own; it's not hard.) Gentlemen may be able to dye an old pair of all-leather chukka boots black (they're much like the men's shoes worn from the 18th Century through the brogans and Civil War booties of later years.) Leather dye is available from sutlers, Tandy Leather Company, or from your local shoe-repair shop. From the late 18th Century up to the Civil War, women often wore some variation of the simple leather slipper. Look for a pair of black flats--with leather soles if possible. In the backwoods, women also wore moccasins or went barefoot. These are temporary solutions, of course (except for the handmade moccasins), but they'll get you off on the right foot (pun intended.)

8. Don't carry everything you own. It isn't necessary to look as though you're on a week-long journey while hanging around the settlements; it gets heavy and you look odd. You don't carry

everything you own now--why would you have, then, unless you were moving your household? If you are camping at an event, remember the difficulty of early-day travel; unless you had packhorses or are on a route that might have had wagon or keelboat travel, the trunks and iron cookware would probably have stayed behind. Many groups that do go into the woods or perform military exercises suggest that their members put on everything they plan to wear or carry, then jump up and down. If it clatters, jingles, or causes you bodily injury, leave it behind. This works regardless of gender; don't weigh yourself down, especially if you are portraying an everyday denizen of a specific site.

9. *Too many* beads may make you look like a refugee from the hippie era. If they'd get caught on the bushes in the woods, don't wear them or save them for ceremonial use.

10. Ask someone whose opinion you trust for advice. You won't look foolish, just interested in improving your interpretation.

11. A friend offers this: If it looks "neat" or "cool," don't buy it. Impulse buying, especially early on, costs us all a nice packet of cash.

12. Point two from this same friend: "If it ain't right, it ain't right"-- and he's right. No amount of rationalizing can make something that wasn't available in 1796 or 1585 or 1812 appropriate just because you like it.

Many of these ideas may sound familiar; you probably know most of them. But we *all* continue to learn, polishing and refining our clothing and gear, all the time. We give away or trade or sell our old stuff that doesn't quite fit our understanding of our persona. Then a few years down the line when we see something that works better--or we change personas--we do it again. We evolve. On the way, you can help someone else who's just getting started. But for both your sakes, make sure you do it from the basis of sound research, not just something passed around the rendezvous circuit. There's always an old Graybeard around to offer advice and council, much of it good. Some advice, however, is of the "there were no white women at rendezvous" school. (Check the wives of missionaries who were at the 1838 rendezvous at Pope Agie, which advertised "come·to the Rendezvous--plenty of whiskey and white women"--much to the disappointment of the trappers.)

## *Meanwhile, here are some basics of clothing:*

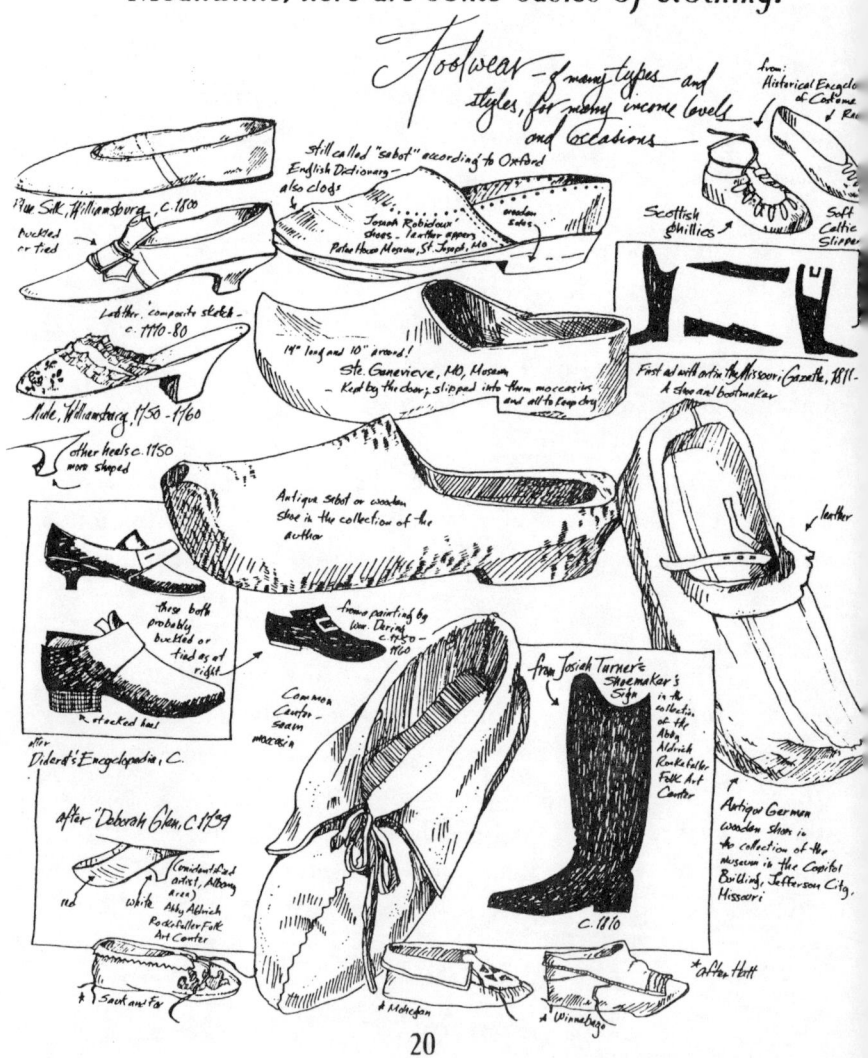

Footwear—of many types and styles, for many income levels and occasions

from: Historical Encyclopedia of Costume & Fashion

Still called "sabot" according to Oxford English Dictionary also clods

Josiah Robidoux shoes - leather uppers Patee House Museum, St. Joseph, Mo.

wooden soles

Scottish ghillies!

Soft Celtic Slipper

17 in. Silk, Williamsburg, C. 1800 buckled or tied

Leather, composite sketch c. 1770-80

14" long and 10" around! Ste. Genevieve, Mo. Museum - Kept by the door; slipped into them moccasins and all to keep dry

First ad with artist the Missouri Gazette, 1811. A shoe and bootmaker

Mule, Williamsburg, 1750 - 1760

other heels c. 1750 more shaped

Antique sabot or wooden shoe in the collection of the author

leather

these both probably buckled or tied as at right.

from painting by Wm. Deering c. 1760-1800

from Josiah Turner's Shoemaker's Sign in the collection of the Abby Aldrich Rockefeller Folk Art Center

stacked heel

Common Center seam moccasin

after Diderot's Encyclopedia, C.

Antique German wooden shoe in the collection of the museum in the Capitol Building, Jefferson City, Missouri

after "Deborah Glen, C.1739

(Unidentified artist, Albany area) Abby Aldrich Rockefeller Folk Art Center

red

white

C. 1810

*after Hoff

* Sack and Fox

* Mohegan

* Winnebago

20

# This undergarment had several names:

## Shift, Smock (Irish) Chemise (French and upper class designation by 19th C.), Shimmy

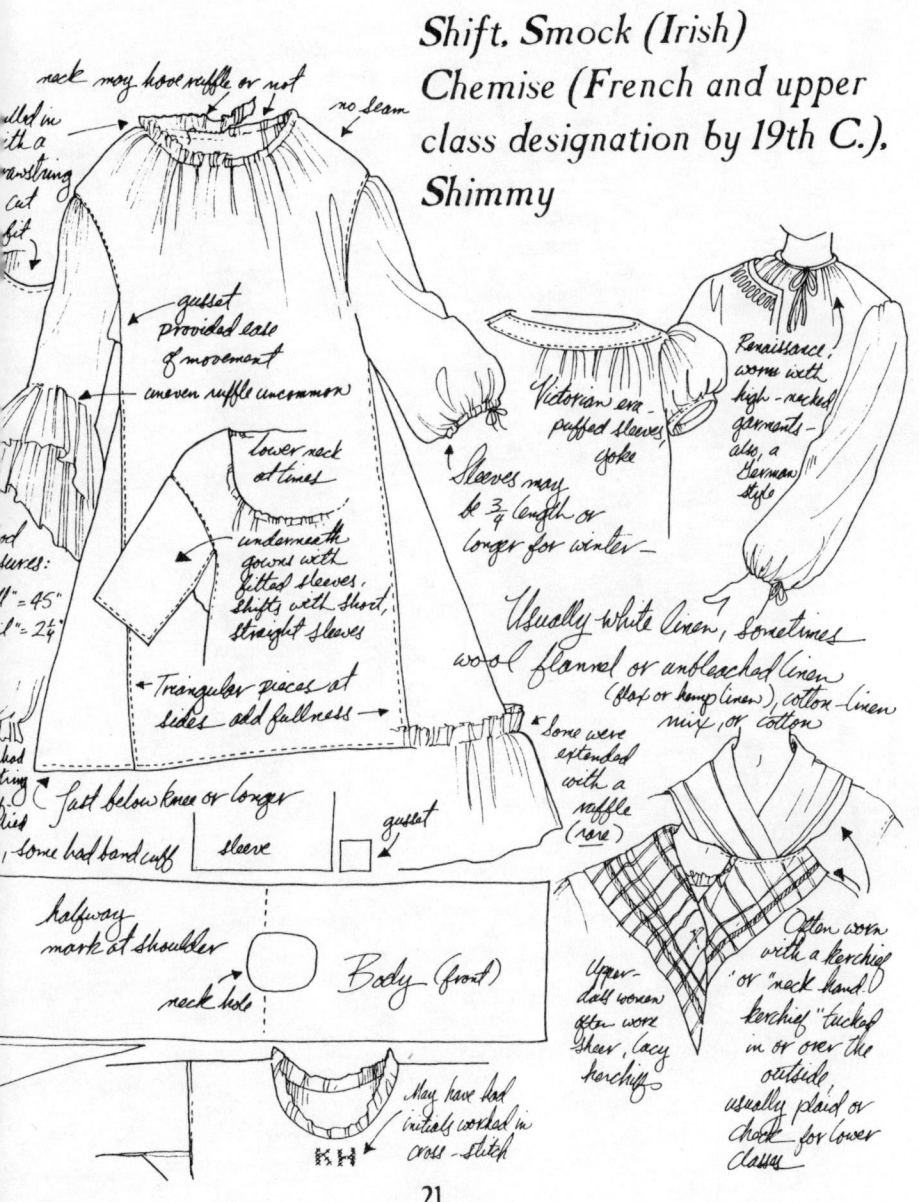

nack may have ruffle or not

no seam

...lled in ...ith a ...rawstring ...cut ...fit

gusset provided ease of movement

uneven ruffle uncommon

lower neck at times

underneath gowns with fitted sleeves, shifts with short, straight sleeves

Triangular pieces at sides add fullness

...d
...eeves:
1" = 45"
1" = 2¼"

...had
...ting
...ied

fell below knee or longer

some had band cuff

sleeve

gusset

halfway mark at shoulder

neck hole

Body (front)

K H

May have had initials worked in cross-stitch

Victorian era puffed sleeves, yoke

Renaissance: worn with high-necked garments - also, a German style

Sleeves may be ¾ length or longer for winter

Usually white linen, sometimes wool flannel or unbleached linen (flax or hemp linen), cotton-linen mix, or cotton

Some were extended with a ruffle (rare)

Upper-class women often wore sheer, lacy kerchiefs

Often worn with a kerchief or "neck band" kerchief tucked in or over the outside, usually plaid or check for lower classes

21

neck gusset

Back almost uniformly gathered at neck

Not a seam — just shoulder reinforcement

Heart or triangle typical

Some shirts had the owner's initials here or at hem

Band collar

Slit at bottom, with gusset for strength

tuck shirt is 1840s, 1850, probably

the basic shape didn't change in 18th and 19th Centuries —

Tow, linen, bleached linen, oznaburg — overshirt of linen or wool

Smocks worn by European farmers for protection

After W.H. Pyne "Microcosm"

gusset

Some shirts have fancy needlework

Long to stay tucked in, double as night shirt

BACK

slit for back

neck gussets

shoulder reinforcement (optional)

FRONT

Fringed bottom

sleeve

cuff

gusset

Basic neck and sleeve — gathers to fit

Fancy dress shirt — still basic square shape, but ruffles at neck (and perhaps at cuff)

Turned-back cuff is 19th C. style

cuff treatment

some used cuff

# Westkits (or Waistcoats), Coats, Greatcoats, etc.

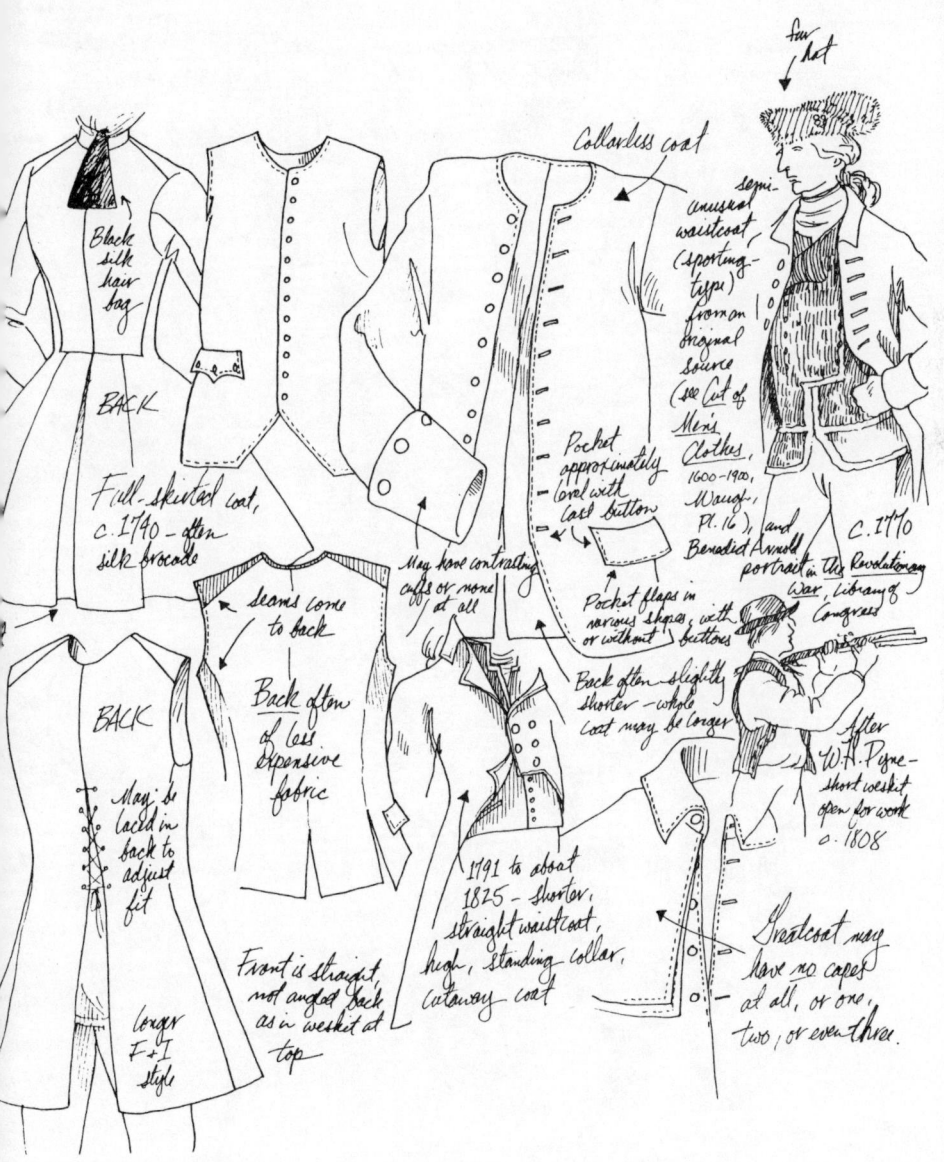

Black silk hair bag

BACK

Full-skirted coat, c. 1740 - often silk brocade

seams come to back

Back often of less expensive fabric

BACK

May be laced in back to adjust fit

Longer F+I style

Front is straight, not angled back as in weskit at top

1791 to about 1825 - shorter, straight waistcoat, high, standing collar. Cutaway coat

Collarless coat

Pocket approximately oval with cast button

May have contrasting cuffs or none at all

Pocket flaps in various shapes, with or without buttons

Back often slightly shorter - whole coat may be longer

fur hat

semi-unusual waistcoat (sporting-type) from an original source (see Cut of Men's Clothes, 1600-1900, Waugh, Pl. 16), and Benedict Arnold portrait in the Revolutionary War, Library of Congress

c. 1770

After W.H. Pyne - short weskit open for work c. 1808

Greatcoat may have no capes at all, or one, two, or even three

23

# Shortgowns and Bedgowns

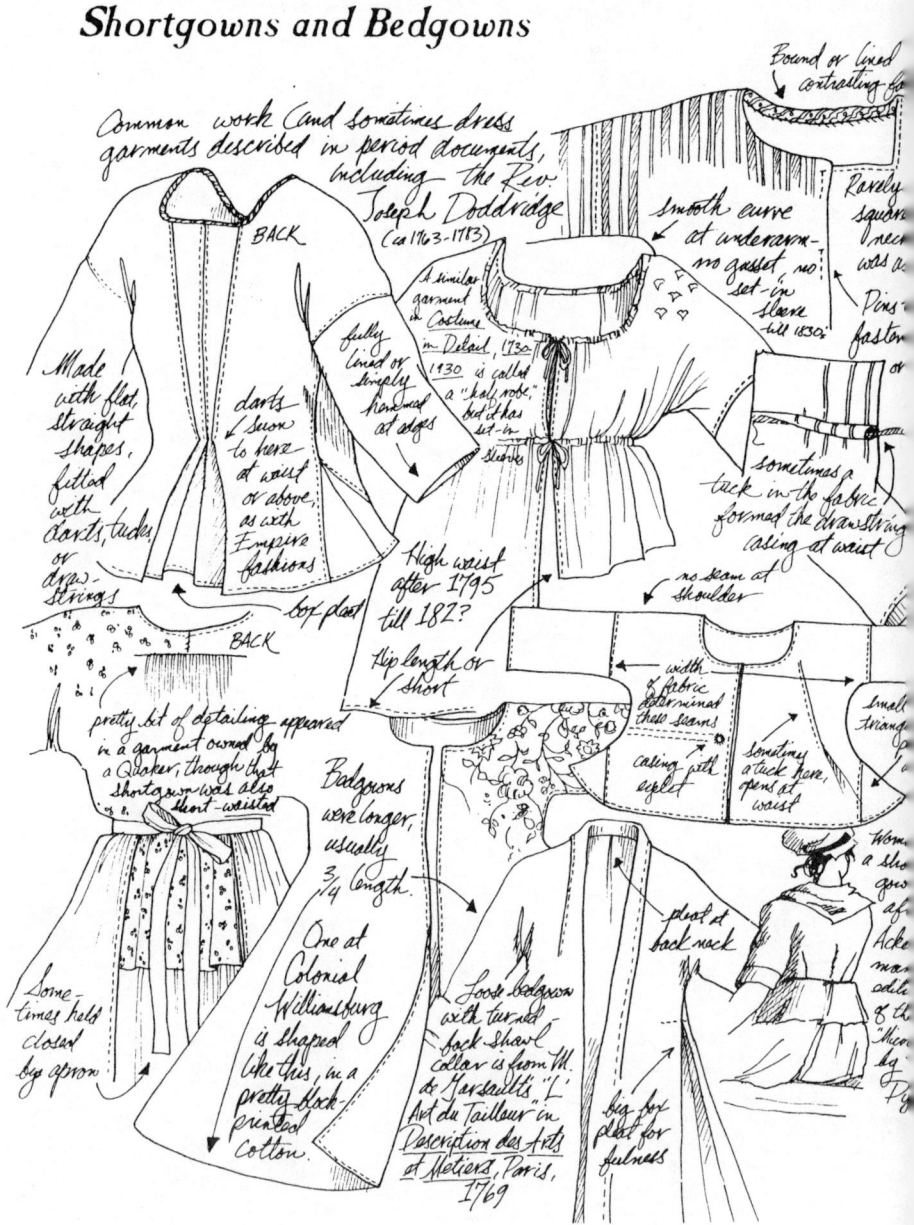

Common work (and sometimes dress garments described in period documents, including the Rev. Joseph Doddridge (ca 1763-1783)

BACK

Bound or lined contrasting

Rarely square neck was a

Pins fasten or

smooth curve at underarm — no gusset, no set-in sleeve till 1830s

A similar garment in Costume in Detail, 1730. 1730 is called a "half-robe," but it has set-in sleeve

Made with flat, straight shapes, fitted with darts, tucks, or draw-strings

darts sewn to here at waist or above, as with Empire fashions

fully lined or simply hemmed at edges

High waist after 1795 till 182?

Hip length or short

box pleat

BACK

sometimes a tuck in the fabric formed the drawstring casing at waist

no seam at shoulder

width of fabric determined these seams

pretty bit of detailing appeared in a garment owned by a Quaker, though that shortgown was also short-waisted

Bedgowns were longer, usually 3/4 length.

casing with eyelet

sometimes a tuck here, opens at waist

small triang

One at Colonial Williamsburg is shaped like this, in a pretty block-printed cotton

Some-times held closed by apron

Loose bedgown with turned back shawl collar is from M. de Garsault's "L' Art du Tailleur" in Description des Arts et Métiers, Paris, 1769

pleat at back neck

big box pleat for fulness

Wom a sho gow af Acke ma sdle g th "theor by P

24

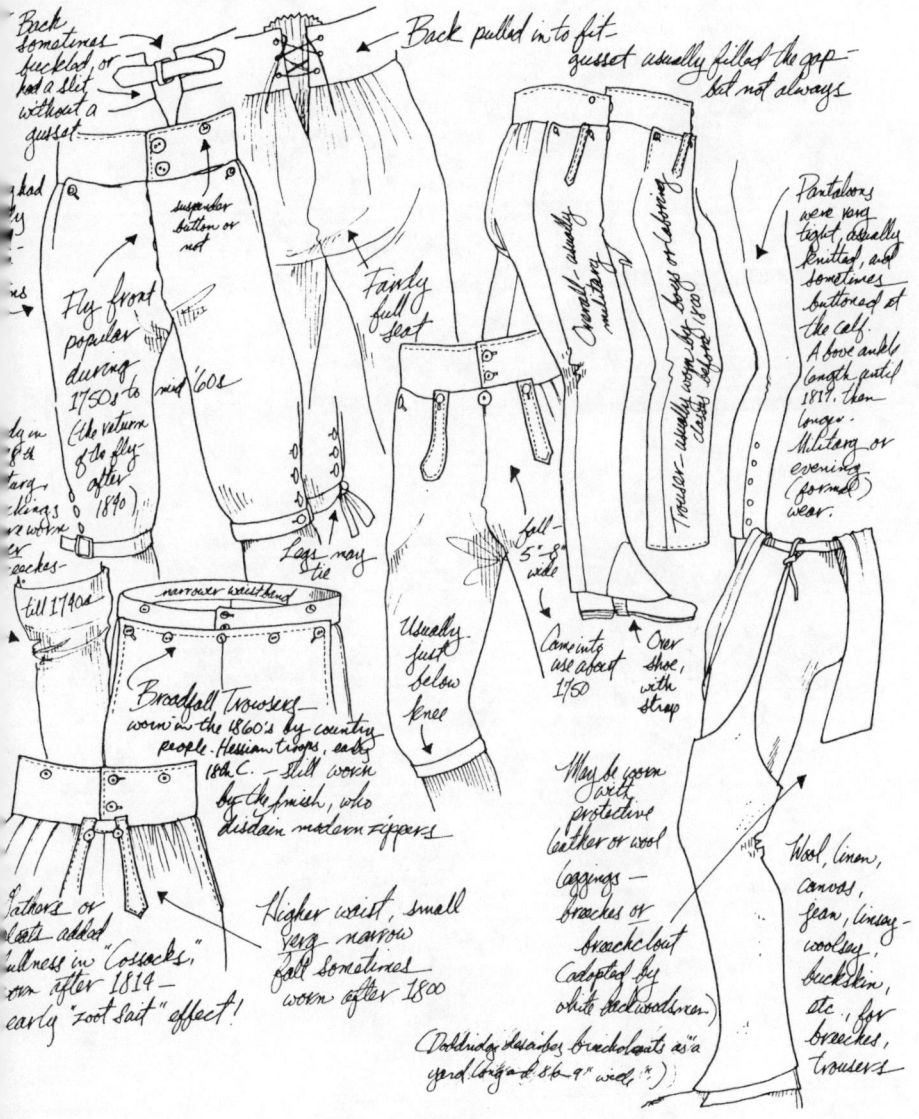

Back sometimes buckled, or had a slit without a gusset

had fly

us

Fly front popular during 1750s to mid '60s (the return of the fly after 1840)

till 1740s

da in 8d targ- kings re worn r eaches

Back pulled in to fit

suspender button or not

Fairly full seat

Legs may tie

Usually just below knee

gusset usually filled the gap — but not always

Overalls usually military

Trowser—usually worn over boots or leggings, closely defined leg

Came into use about 1750

fall 5"-8" wide

Over shoe with strap

Pantaloons were very tight, usually knitted, and sometimes buttoned at the calf. Above ankle length until 1817, then longer. Military or evening (formal) wear.

narrower waistband

Broadfall Trowsers worn in the 1860's by country people. Hessian troops, early 18th C. — still worn by the Amish, who disdain modern zippers

Gathers or pleats added fullness in "Cossacks," even after 1814 — early "zoot suit" effect!

Higher waist, small very narrow fall sometimes worn after 1800

May be worn with protective leather or wool leggings — breeches or breechclout (adopted by white backwoodsmen)

(Doddridge describes breechclouts as "a yard long and 8 to 9" wide.")

Wool, linen, canvas, jean, linsey-woolsey, buckskin, etc. for breeches, trousers

25

# Petticoats and Aprons

May have had buttons, hook and eye, or tie closings

may be gathered,   stroke gathered,   or pleated

often 2 widths of fabric used until 19th C. fashion dictated extremes of fullness

Wool, linen, linsey-woolsey, or more rarely, cotton or silk

In winter, under petticoats were often quilted for warmth.

Polonaise-style gown over petticoat

May have tucks to adjust length or for decoration

Aprons had ties threaded through a casing...

...or a binding or band at the waist. Some had tops

They were sometimes embroidered silk for dress,

worn high with Empire styles...

these were called pinners, for obvious reasons

or looped up and tucked into waist (or "kilted") for carrying things in.

Ankle-length petticoat (Shorter lengths stayed cleaner, stayed out of the fire, and lasted longer — not so likely to drag and wear out your hem.)

...or above — (Peter Kalm said the French wore them quite a bit above in 1757.)

Slaves and indentured servants often wore matching shortgowns and petticoats as fabric was bought by the bolt for servants. Their mistresses were more likely to mix fabrics (though several period paintings show slaves in equally mixed attire.)

Slits o ...de wea ... get ... her ... po ... bo ... lik ... cl ... p ... w ... a ... x

Pocke

26

# ⚜HISTORICAL NOTES⚜

When in doubt, go to primary documents for information on what was done and by whom, what was worn, used, or eaten, and when it was available--and in common use. Journals, diaries, advertisements for runaways, inventories, etc. are wonderful sources, as are period engravings or sketches. (Later illustrations may have been romanticized or simply the result of lazy research--they *can* be good sources if you're familiar with the basics.) Here are a few taken from a variety of sources which demonstrate the types of information that can be gleaned. Some are from "my" territory, which covered a huge area and a long period of time, and others are from Canada and back east.

**Pennsylvania, New Jersey, 1685:** "... Schools [should] be provided in all Towns and Cities, and persons of known honesty, skill and understanding be yearly chosen by the Governor and General Assembly, to teach and instruct Boys and Girls in all the most useful Arts and Sciences that they in their youthful capacities may be capable to understand, as the learning to *Read* and *Write true English, Latine,* and other useful Speeches and Languages, and *fair Writing, Arithmetick* and *Bookkeeping...*" (Budd 43)

**East Coast, mid 1700s:** "... The people spin and weave a great part of their everyday apparel and dye it in their houses. Flax is cultivated by many people and succeeds very well, but hemp is not used here" (Kalm 185). He may have meant on the east coast/Pennsylvania, NY, etc., since hemp was apparently woven elsewhere.

**New Hampshire, 1757:** from "*The Captivity of Mrs. Johnson,*" "We were roused by neighbor Labarree's knocking at the door ... Mr.

Johnson slipped on his Jacket and trowsers[4], and stepped to the door to let him in." Then, during the capture: "On viewing myself I found that I . . . was naked. An Indian had plundered three gowns, who, on seeing my situation, gave me the whole. I asked another for a petticoat[5], but he refused it." (Johnson 27-28)

Don't overlook unexpected sources; in the writings of another culture we may find tidbits to tell us about our own. Here, the French Baron de Carondelet, Governor of Louisiana, writes of the menace of American expansion into French territory:

Louisiana Territory, 1793: "This vast and restless popluation, driving the Indian tribes continually before them and upon us, is endeavoring to gain all the vast continent . . . The wandering spirit, and the ease with which these people procure their support and shelter, form new settlements readily. A carbine and a little cornmeal in a sack is sufficient for an American to range the forests alone for a month. With this carbine he kills wild cattle and deer for food, and protects himself from the savages. Having dampened the cornmeal, it serves in lieu of bread. He erects a house by laying some tree trunks across others in the form of a square; and even a fort impregnable to the savages, by building on a story crosswise above the ground floor. The cold does not fright him, and when a family grows tired of one place, it moves to another . . . ." (Houck, Spanish

---

[4] Generally recognized to be long pants as opposed to knee-length breeches. Often worn by boys or for work.

[5] A petticoat is a garment we might call a skirt. May be worn in multiples, one on top of another with the top layer tucked up; with a jacket or short gown, or under a gown of the French or English style. More rarely, with stays and chemise alone.

Regime, II, 12, 13). From this we can pick a variety of facts: That the Americans were very self-sufficient; that they had continued moving Westward agressively; that cornmeal was considered a necessity; that log homes were being build and fortified; and that women and children were part of the picture, among other things.

Inventories are invaluable sources for information on material culture--what people had and used. The discoveries are sometimes more than a little enlightening. One inventory from the estate of the deceased Jacques Bourdon in Kaskaskia in July of 1723 included:

> 1 old hunting horn
> 1 bullet mold
> 14 guns and one musket
> 200 gun flints
> 9 dozen and 8 knives *a Chien de Corne*, 10 Flemish
>         knives, 2 woodcutter's knives
> 40 pounds of lead balls
> 1 pair of pocket pistols
> 2 barrels of powder weighing 100 pounds each

Among other more domestic items were a cot, a peppermill, and "2 miserable scythes." This man was well prepared.

Another inventory from this same source, this time of a woman, Marie Catherine Baron, who died in July of 1748, also included a cot, along with a hunting knive, a silver pistol, and her own bullet mold among her more expected household belongings (Belting 43-46).

Journals are often often good sources. It's neccesary to take attitude into consideration, since the more educated travelers may have been shocked by what they saw. However, because the backwoods or Colonial inhabitants were often unusual to them, they noted what they saw in some detail. We are the beneficiaries.

**Carolinas, 1740s:** "In summer, they [the Indians of the Carolinas] feed much on vegetables, particularly maize before it is ripe, and while tender, they roast it in the fire, also pumpkins, gourds, squashes, melons, cucumners [sic], potatoes; besides peaches, raspberries and strawberries, which their woods abound in. Indians seldom plant corn enough to last them the year round, yet in some measure they supply that want by their autumn collection of black walnuts, hickory nuts, chinkapins and acorns, which they lay up for winter store; from these they press wholesome oil, particularly from the acorns of the live oak. The kernals also of these nuts and acorns being beat in a mortar to a paste, serve to thicken and enrich their broths.

"Besides roasting and boiling, they barbecue most of the flesh of the larger animals, such as buffalo, bear and deer; this performed very gradually, over a slow clear fire, upon a large wooden gridiron, raised two feet above the fire. By this method of curing venison it will keep good five or six weeks .... It is common with some nations at great entertainments, to boil bear, deer, panther or other animals, together in the same pot; they take out the bones, and serve up the meat by itself, then they stew out the bones over again in the same liquor, adding thereto purslane and squashes, and thicken it with the tender grain of maize, this is a luscious soup ....The pigeons afford them some years great plenty of oil, which they preserve for winter use; this and sometimes bear's fat they eat with bread .... They thicken their broths with *roccahomony*, which is indeed, for that purpose, much preferable to oatmeal or French barley" (Catesby 146).

**East Coast, Mid 1700s:** " . . .The persimmon, or *Diospyros Virginiana* L. grew in the marshy fields and about pools. Its little apples looked very well, but are not fit for eating before the frost has affected them and then they have a fine taste. Hesselius gathered some of them and desired my servant to taste of this fruit of the land, but the poor credulous fellow had hardly bit into them when he felt the qualities they have before the frost has touched them, for they contracted his mouth so that he could hardly speak and got a very disagreeable taste. This disgusted him so much that he was with difficulty persuaded to taste of it during the whole of our stay in America . . . "(Kalm 36-37).

Virginia, Pennsylvania, 1763-1783: The Rev. Joseph Doddridge on clothing: "The hunting shirt was universally worn. This was a kind of loose frock[6], reaching halfway down the thighs, with large sleeves, open before, and so wide as to lap over a foot or more when belted. The cap[e] was large, and sometimes handsomely fringed with a ravelled piece of cloth of a different color from that of the hunting shirt itself. The bosom . . . served as a wallet to hold a hunk of bread, cakes, jerk, tow for wiping the barrel of the rifle, or any other necessary . . . The belt, which was always tied behind, answered several purposes, besides that of holding the dress together. In cold weather the mittens, and sometimes the bullet-bag, occupied the front part of it. To the right side was suspended the tomahawk, and to the left the scalping knife in its leathern sheath. The hunting shirt was generally made of linsey, sometimes of coarse linen, and a few of dressed deer skins . . . The shirt and jacket were of the common fashion. A pair of drawers or breeches and leggins[7] were the dress of

---

[6] A looser, country-style informal coat, simpler in cut than formal coats of the early 1700s; i.e., a "hunting frock." Only became known as an article of women's clothing synonymous with a dress later, in the 19th C.

[7] Leggings were a snugly-fitted covering from the ankle to the knee or thigh; made of wool or leather. They may have buttoned, tied, or simply be made to pull on and fasten to the belt with ties.

the thigh and legs; a pair of moccasins[8] answered for the feet much better than shoes. These were made of dressed deer skin. They were mostly made of a single piece with a gathering seam along the top of the foot, and another from the bottom of the heel, without gathers as high as the ankle joint or a little higher. Flaps were left on each side to reach some distance up the leg. They were nicely adapted to the ankles and lower part of the leg by thongs of deer skin so that no dust, gravel or snow could get within the moccasin...."

Doddridge also describes the common dress of women, the "linsey petticoat and bed gown[9] ... which were the universal dress of our women ... they went barefooted in warm weather, and in cold their feet were covered with moccasins, coarse shoes or shoepacks.[10]

"In the later years of the Indian war our young men became more enamored of the Indian dress throughout, with the exception of the matchcoat. The drawers were laid aside and leggins made longer, so as to reach the upper part of the thigh. The Indian breech clout was adopted. This was a piece of linen or cloth nearly a yard long, and eight or nine inches broad. This passed under the belt before and behind leaving the ends for flaps hanging before and behind over the belt ... strings which supported the long leggins were attached. When this belt, as was often the case, passed over the hunting shirt the upper

---

[8] Moccasins were mentioned in many period documents as footwear easily obtained in the backwoods, either by trading with the Indians or by home manufacture and worn by both sexes.

[9] Bedgowns weren't worn to bed; they were common work clothing, an unfitted coat-like garment worn well into the mid-19th century.

[10] Shoepacks were a kind of cross between moccasins and European-style shoes. Often used for winter wear and lined with wool.

part of the thighs and part of the hips were naked.

"The young warrior instead of being abashed by this nudity was proud of his Indian like dress. In some instances I have seen them go into places of public worship in this dress. Their appearance however, did not add much to the devotion of the young ladies" (Doddridge 91-93). Talk about understatement!

**Louisiana Territory, 1797:** Lest you imagine this is a strictly eastern phenomenon, rest assured that Nicolas de Finiels, the French engineer assigned to the Louisiana Territory from 1797 through 1803 mentions the same fashion. "They were compelled to adopt many Indian customs and clothing styles: the breechclout took the place of culottes[11]; leggings replaced stockings; doeskin moccasins succeeded European shoes; a loose-fitting tunic covered the rest of the body; a blue kerchief wrapped about the head completed the costume. When cold weather renders this dress inadequate, a cloak of bergopzoom[12] or rough blue fabric, fitted with a hood, protects the body. Some persons don fur hats that cover the necks and ears, and a pair of fur mittens attached by a long string that passes over the shoulders like a stole; the mittens hang down on either side in case your hands need protection, but when not required they are out of the way without any danger of being . . . lost. [Author's note: This is the same arrangement of mittens required of Rogers' Rangers as a lifesaving measure.] With this simple outfit you can move easily through the

---

[11] "Culotte" is the French equivalent for the English breeches. Waugh, *The Cut of Men's Clothes*, Pg. 90

[12] According to James Pitot, bergopzoom was the same as "laced calmont." Closest fabric name in *Textiles in America, 1650-1870*, is Calmuc, a twilled woolen with a long nap used for winter dress goods, which seem to match the descriptions of bergopzoom or bergopsom.

woods, tracking deer, wildcats, and wild turkeys . . ." (de Finiels 112).

Describing the dress of women in this French territory, de Finiels says: "Female costumes have the same simplicity: a skirt of blue gingham and a short calico vest in the summer or wool in the winter; a sort of long cotton cloak . . . ; a blue or sometimes white kerchief knotted over the forehead, the other two corners of which hang down behind the head; this constitutes daily dress.

*after*
*Anna Maria*
*Von Phul, 1818*

"Calico dresses with dyed designs, and some silk dresses in the antique style that suggest a bit of opulence, make up holiday clothes" (de Finiels 113). However, a few pages later, he recants a bit concerning French simplicity: "Young women and maids already disdain the costumes of the mothers and have relegated them to old age for covering their wrinkles and the ravages of time. Embroidered muslin, tarlatan, fine and brilliant silk, and lawn cloth have replaced modest cotton, printed calico and bergopzoom. Elegant corsets gallantly delineate waistlines that were once covered by jackets and suggest the seductive figures that they scarcely conceal. . . . " (Ibid. 115).

**Indiana, 1797:** Benjamin Henry Latrobe sketched a barefoot backwoods family--a mother in ragged, high-waisted dress and three children, all in what appear to be poke-style bonnets--including the boy. He also drew women in shortgowns[13] and petticoats and people

---

[13] Shortgowns were also common work garments, perhaps originally literally cut "short" from worn gowns. Later, they were jacket-like, without set-in sleeves, and from just below waist-length to hip length. They pinned or tied shut at the natural waist (or above, during Regency period.)

34

playing billiards, one man wearing knee breeches and a cutaway coat, while another is barefoot, in shirt sleeves and baggy trowsers. One gentleman wrapped his shins in blankets "to discourage mosquitos."

after a
Self-Portrait
Sketch by John
James Audubon
1826

Kentucky, Tennessee, Louisiana and Missouri Territory, 1811-1812: Audubon came to the Missouri Territory to open a store at Ste. Genevieve. He described his travels in some detail, and drew a self-portrait in his woodsman's gear--buckskins, leggings, long rifle, and other accoutrements (Ford, editor, Pl. 6).

He also describes meeting Daniel Boone in Kentucky and accompanying him on a hunting trip: "...My companion, a stout, hale, and athletic man, dressed in a homespun hunting shirt, bare-legged and moccasined, carried a long and heavy rifle, which, as he was loading it, he said had proved efficient in all his former undertakings, and which he hoped would not fail on this occasion, as he felt proud to show me his skill" (Audubon 62).

Missouri Territory, 1808: On his way from the east to outfit the factory at Ft. Osage, George Sibley writes: "Saturday 28th--Bot. 30 pieces tincel lace ... Also bot. Several articles for my own use. A

Coat, Pantaloons[14] ... etc." Later, Sibley says: "pd. A tailor $5.471/2 for making a Flannel Coatee, pair of drawers[15], & a Morning Gown & . . . Buttons, & C." ( Sibley's unpublished diary, Missouri Historical Society, St. Louis; transcript 2).

Missouri Territory, 1810: . . . "We have been accompanied for these two days past, by a man and two lads; ascending in a canoe . . . These people are well dressed in handsome home-made cotton cloth. The man seemed to possess no small share of pride and self importance, which, as I afterwards discovered, arose from his being a captain of militia" (Brackenridge 39).

Missouri Territory 1818: Henry Rowe Schoolcraft describes backwoods dress in the Missouri Territory: "The dress of the children attracted our attention. The boys were clothed in a particular kind of garment made of deer-skin, which served the double purpose of shirt and jacket. The girls had buck-skin frocks, which it was evident, by the careless manner in which they were clothed, were intended to combine the utility both of linen and calico, and all were abundantly greasy and dirty (Schoolcraft 69).

Later, describing another backwoods family which had a few more advantages, education and comfort: "Some part of the wearing

---

[14] Pantaloons were extremely tight long pants often worn by the military or for evening wear. Calf length until 1817, then longer. (Waugh, *Cut of Men's Clothes,* Pg. 116) However, those shown in *Revolution in Fashion* look looser, more like trousers. (Pg. 77)

[15] Drawers were defined as summer breeches in *History of American Costume,* Book I, 1607-1800 by Elizabeth McClellan, Tudor Publishing, p 622; elsewhere as underwear.

apparel of himself and family was of foreign manufacture" (Schoolcraft 81). Again, describing another family recently migrated to the Territory: "The girls are brought up with little care ... Being deprived of all the advantages of dress, possessed by our fair countrywomen in the east, they are by no means calculated to inspire admiration, but on the contrary disgust; their whole wardrobe, until the age of twelve, consisting of one greasy buckskin frock, which is renewed whenever worn out" (Schoolcraft 104). He also mentions that furs were exchanged for "flour, salt, and whiskey, with some coffee, *calico*, and a few smaller articles" (Schoolcraft 142).

**Kentucky, Indiana, 1832:** There are several examples of European clothing in *Karl Bodmer's America*, in addition to a wealth of Native American stuff. "Backwoods Man and Woman on Horseback" (Hunt and Gallagher 84) depicts a man in short jacket and top hat and a woman in slat or poke bonnet; the sketchy "Taking on Wood in Rainy Weather," (Hunt and Gallagher 105) shows men with top hats, capote[16]-like garments or tail coats, shirts and trousers. Latrobe had painted people in capotes of white material with blue stripes in 1819 in his sketch of "Market folks" (Carter, Van Horne and Brownell 357). "The Hunter Russell," done near New Harmony, Indiana, wears a ragged shirt with a torn elbow and large collar tucked into what appear to be baggy-seated fall-front trousers, with a hunting bag, large powder horn with a prominent plug, and rifle or musket over his

---

[16] The most common definition is a blanket-coat. There were many styles from the early coat cut on the more formal style to the one we recognize as a capote today. Interestingly, C.C. Robin mentions in 1805 that the capotes worn by slaves were the only ones with a hood. Interestingly, *capote* also defined as a woman's hat or bonnet, shaped like a morning glory flower. (Kyoto Fashion Institute, various editors 162).

shoulder. He wears a dark slouch hat. (Hunt and Gallagher 122).

Louisiana Territory: A 20th-Century history of Missouri describes
the clothing of the latter half of 18th and early 19th C.; this would
have still been Spanish and/or French territory until 1803, when the
United States acquired the huge Louisiana Territory that virtually
doubled the size of the United States: "Clothes worn by most of the
people were made of materials readily available--cotton, wool, linen,
and skins. The average man wore his long hair fixed in a queue and
bound in an eelskin around which was wound a kerchief in summer.
In winter he wore a kind of stocking cap. He was dressed in a cotton
or woolen shirt or blouse of a bright color or plaid, a pair of cotton
pantaloons or leather breeches held up by a leather belt with pouches
for knives and tobacco. He might be wearing a pair of leggings, while
on his feet he wore Indian sandals or moccasins. The most unique
part of this dress was a long coat of a coarse blanket cloth with a cape
or hood (capot) which could be put over his head in cold or rainy
weather. Sometimes the hood was of fur or deerskin."

   Describing the clothing of women, March says: "The men
were quite willing for their wives and daughters to dress much more
attractively than they. The woman wore a blue kerchief on her head,
no hat . . . and walked in moccasins or Indian sandals. An apron made
of deerskin might be worn . . . For special occasions . . .Those who
could afford it dressed . . . in garments of silk, satin, taffeta, or velvet.
Gentlemen indulged in clothes of many colors, expensive waistcoats
with braid, coats and breeches decorated with ornamental buttons, and
slippers with silver buckles. Silk ribbons were worn in their queues,
and the hair was powdered. Their women wore corsets, lace fichus,
silk scarves, silk or satin dresses, ribbons, ivory or horn combs in
their hair, earrings, silk stockings, and fine leather slippers, imported
from France or New Orleans. It has been said that fashions of Paris
reached the French in Missouri more quickly than European models
reached the eastern seaboard states. Certainly, St. Louis and the other
towns in Upper Louisiana were no miniature replicas of Paris, but

38

neither were their inhabitants semi-savages wrapped in blankets." (March 113).

It should be noted that this passage applies to Americans as well as to the French. Period maps and documents indicate that there were Americans as well as British living in the Illinois Country, Spanish and French Louisiana, and the lands that became the Missouri Territory. In 1797, de Finiels noted the proportion of French to Americans, Indians and Blacks living in every town he mentioned, along with notations on merchants and the few craftsmen in the area. One must assume the Americans did business with these same convenient craftsmen and merchants; their advertisements appear in the newspapers of the time.

Timber framing the
carpenter's shop at
Fort Osage

## "I DON'T KNOW WHAT TO *DO!*"
### A List of 78 Suggested Living History Interpreters' Roles, Duties, and Demonstrations

Now that you have an idea of who you are and what you want to wear, you need something to do. Of course, that's usually not a problem--your activities grow naturally out of your persona.

This list came about sometime after my husband and I started volunteering at Missouri's Fort Osage. He was at loose ends--in short, *bored* (as difficult as that might be for some of us to imagine!)--but then this is *my* hobby, not his. So, in response to his question as to what might he do, I researched this list. All activities are appropriate for the time period of the early 1700s through the mid 1800s and can, for the most part, be done by men or women.

That's an important point. Unfortunately, some women have been told there's nothing for them to do but be camp followers (with the inference that the term might mean a woman of loose morals)-- lazy research, that, or none at all! Even in a military camp there's room for variety in interpretation and activities. This list is also intended to open the door to the possibilities for all of us; if some of the less-practiced activities are chosen, it only broadens our understanding and interpretation of the past. Not everyone can or should be a ranger, scout or longhunter. Remember, there were tradesmen (and tradeswomen, including tinsmiths like Mrs. S. Pencill, of Charlestown, South Carolina) (Kauffman 110), innkeepers, explorers, tarts, doctors, artists, farmers, settlers, sutlers, tailors, boatmen, pirates, banditti and others throughout the colonies and on the frontier, which at one time encompassed the lands that stretched from Pennsylvania to Ohio to the Illinois/Louisiana/Missouri Territory and beyond.

Pick what you will, if you're just getting started--or if you're looking for a new direction after a few years in living history. This list is intended as a jumping-off point only; there are many more possible activities.

☞Artist (Remember Thomas Say, William Bartram, the Peale family, Benjamin Latrobe, Lewis Miller, Audubon, Anna Maria Von Phul, Liwwat Boke, etc. All artists weren't professionals; some just drew for their own enjoyment, or as an adjunct to their work as military tacticians, spies, mapmakers, naturalists or whatever.) *Astronomical observation (as a scientist, farmer, sailor or witch) * Basket making (collect your own materials) * Beading/bead-making (quill, glass, pottery, crinoid, shell) * Blacksmithing * Bookbinding * Bookkeeping (trade room, office, sutler's tent) * Botanical collections (Remember the Bartrams, Mark Catesby, Jane Colden, John James Audubon, John Bradbury, Thomas Nuttall, etc.) note-taking, sketching plants. * Box, carton, or container-making * Bread-baking * Brewing * Butchering/salting meat * Candle making * Carving (wood, bone, etc.) * Celebrating (i.e., Audubon's account of a Kentucky celebration) * Construction (carpentry, timber-framing, joinery) * Cooking (simple or elaborate) * Cross-stitch (marking clothing or blankets, or young girls making samplers) * Digging (gardens, holes, fishing worms) * Dispensing liquor to militia * Doctoring * Dyeing with natural dyes--clothing, quills, etc. * Eating (always a favorite; research table manners--if any.) * Fence building--or fencing! * Fire starting (demonstrate various ways, materials, tinders) * Floorcloth-making * Games (lacrosse, tug of war, graces, races, cards, draughts [checkers], quoits, etc.) * Garden chores, drying fruits or vegetables for winter * Gathering wild plants (for dyeing, cooking, medicinals) * Glass blowing * Guide (period first person or present-day) * Hanging clothes--on fences, bushes, or on a line * Hearing confessions (this requires specialized clothing!) * Herb gardening, dispensing, lore * Housecleaning (dusting, straightening, scrubbing floors) * Hunting * Ironing/starching/sun-bleaching * Knitting * Lead casting (balls, spoons, buttons, etc.) * Leather work (repair or new) * Madwoman (or man) (Brackenridge mentions such a woman) * Making dugout or birchbark canoes * Making moccasins (period paintings or engravings show the proper style for your area of the country) * Making paper (from rags, weeds, straw, etc.) * Making quill or reed pens * Mantua-making * Mending (sails, clothing, moccasins, guns, horns, etc.) * Midwifery (including a familiarity with herbs and cures) * Military duty (there are plenty of groups, from the Missouri Rangers to the Brigade of the American Revolution.) * Militia duty (a more casual interpretation than the former) * Music-making, singing, dancing * Painting or whitewashing barracks, houses, cabins * Politicians/speechifying * Powderhorn-making (and other horn tools) * Quilting (quilted petticoats and undergarments for winter) * Reading (even in the backwoods, some people had books; a few inventories show rather extensive libraries by the standards of the day) * Rifle/musket/pistol/cannon shooting and maintenance * Sewing, both mending and new * Shoe-making or repair * Sifting flour to get bugs out * Soap making * Spinning (wool, flax, or silk if you're well-to-do) * Spring or harvest celebrations (especially among cultures recently emigrated) * Surveying * Tanning/smoking/preparing/baling hides * Tatting or bobbin-lace * Teaching (children or adults--reading, writing, shooting skills, tomahawk throwing, mending, catechism, songs, etc.) * Tinware/metalworking * Toy-making * Traders, trade room work, if at a fort site * Trekking (or touring, scouting, voyaging or journeying, as it was called in period documents) * Visiting (this one requires little research) * Washing (clothes, dishes, windows, bodies) * Waterproofing fabric (various techniques) * Weaving (finishing, fulling, etc.) * Wine making * Woodworking; all phases--wooden bowls, gunstocks, small household items, tool handles * Writing (letters, receipts, inventories, journals etc.)

after John James Audubon, 1826 - "Our Capt. Making Powder Flasks" Capt. Jos. Hatch

"Our Carpenter"

2nd Mate

# ℰRESEARCHℰ

**F**inding good sources for research is sometimes confusing. Beginners are not sure where to start, or expect that someone else will have already done it and all they need to do is ask the appropriate museum administrator or librarian. While that's true to an extent (there's no need to reinvent the wheel), you still need to focus your research so you can ask the right questions. Too broad a query will result in no help at all. When I started out, I called Kansas City's Nelson Art Gallery to ask if there were any women artists in early Kansas City and who they were. The answer was: "There were too many to pick out; tell us who you want to know about and we'll help you." Now I know to begin with the history of the area, narrow my focus to women (there are a great many women's history studies these days), *then* look for artists. Or, I'd check period journals for women who sketched their impressions; there are several in local and regional archives.

To help you locate such resources and formulate questions that will actually *help*, we've compiled the following list. Some of the following material appeared in another form in my book, *Living History, Drawing on the Past*. A number of fine researchers, both amateur and professional, contributed to these suggestions. Because this information is so useful, I have added to it and humbly offer it again in this new format.

There are many ways of doing research; remember to include time for fun or you'll become bored and give it up. Watch a movie. Read a historical novel. Talk to knowledgeable friends. Enjoy yourself.

Research terms may be confusing at first; for instance, "tertiary source" is not something you hear every day. It's easy once you become familiar with those terms. When you discover the treasure trove of primary resources you'll be hooked. It's as though someone who actually lived at the time that interests you is telling you all about it, person to person.

*Primary source:* an original document (or reprint): an eyewitness writes about what was going on. It's best if you can find an account written at the time rather than a memoir--memories are sometimes faulty. A participant in a battle, a wilderness traveler, a captive's account are examples of primary sources. Look for journals, account books, duty rosters, indentures, inventories, ads in period newspapers. Many first-person accounts of the New World were written to entice (or discourage) immigrants; it's necessary to take these with the proverbial salt grain.

*Paintings and engravings* can be great resources, especially if they are from the period and not a later time's romantic notions, which may or may not be well researched. (Know your artist, in that case.)

Portraits, as mentioned, are perhaps less helpful than street scenes, landscapes, or depictions of people at work or play--of which there are many. (See Audubon, W.H. Pyne, Lewis Miller, Benjamin Latrobe, Karl Bodmer, etc.) In a portrait the sitter may be in Sunday best, or even wearing garments not their own. Artists, like the photographers who followed, often had a supply of props, including clothing; that's why you may see the same thing on a variety of sitters. It wasn't necessarily slavish fashion, just one of the artist's favorite props. John Singleton Copley painted the vast majority of women wearing no caps, and with the same hairstyle, complete with the *same* strand of pearls in their hair. It's the strand of pearls worn over the decades that makes you realize that Copley just liked that look--and was good at painting pearls!

*Secondary source:* an account written by nonparticipants who have only heard about an event (books, newspaper accounts or the recollections of a relative "back home.") "As-told-to" books and essays, interviews, and quotes are still wonderful sources, but subject to the opinion, the memory, and the slant, political, or otherwise--of the interviewer. Later illustrations, as mentioned, also come under the heading of secondary or tertiary sources.

*Tertiary sources:* Books or magazine articles, even those written hundreds of years after the event, often help put things in perspective. They may explain the overall picture or present a historical overview or interpretation of the facts from the perspective of the Big Picture. These are extremely useful, especially if you are starting out or exploring a new direction; they often contain great lists of resources of primary documents. Again, they are subject to the author's interpretation of history, as are illustrations done by contemporary artists.

*Experiential or experimental research*, also called *experimental archaeology*, with a nod of gratitude to Jay Anderson, author of the *Living History Sourcebook*: this is actually using the tools and accoutrements. You do this every time you go out in the field in period attire. Author\historian Mark Baker has often written of how much he has learned by actually *doing*; his upcoming book will include a great deal of information on this subject. Jay Anderson's works also define the terms and explain how to learn from what you do; see Bibliography for a full listing. Use the same tools and equipment as our forebears and you'll discover for yourself what works and what doesn't. A bit of instruction from someone who has gone this way before you is helpful, but you still learn *for yourself* each time you try your hand.

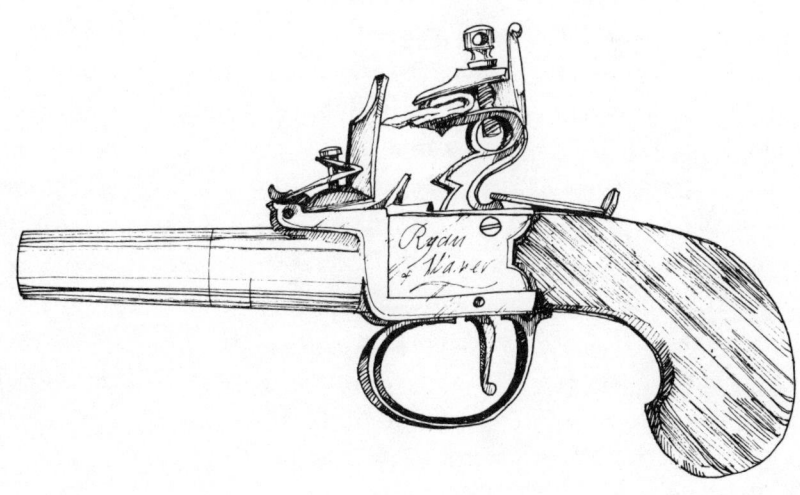

# ✷RESOURCES✷

❧     LIVING HISTORY SITES let you see artifacts or reproductions in action, especially at events with a lot of volunteers. At a site like this you learn by watching, by asking questions, and by doing. Living history programs were designed with this in mind, whether you're at Fort Osage, Conner Prairie, or Colonial Williamsburg. (Even if something looks odd or out of place, though, ask your questions respectfully, not in a confrontational manner. I have found that just because I haven't seen something done, used, or worn before a particular date doesn't mean it didn't happen.) Verify the accuracy, authenticity and appropriateness of the demonstrations you see through asking questions of people whose opinion you trust and by digging on your own; that's half the fun.

    Consider volunteering at the site of your choice. This can be a serious commitment, but a satisfying one. Sites often provide in-depth training sessions and access to their libraries and documents. You may be able to transcribe original documents--what better way to learn?

❧     NATIONAL AND STATE HISTORIC SITES often deal with the casual visitor, but if you need to research in greater depth, make an appointment with the appropriate curator. Send a letter with perhaps five queries which the curator can answer right on your original. Keep queries short, include a self-addressed stamped envelope. You may then set a time for a research expedition, or you may have had your questions answered in the letter itself. A phone call may provide all the information you need; contact the museum or site and ask for the appropriate curator. Many sites now pay special attention to the past as it regards both women and minorities; ask if there is a specific program or curator that might help you. (These sites may also stage reenactments; many have fine libraries.)

❧     MUSEUMS: You may find someone featured that you can base a persona on, or see artifacts your persona might use. If you've made an appointment or have proper credentials, you may get to handle textiles or tools, including those not normally on display. (Be sure to take along white cotton gloves and observe proper museum etiquette--i.e., no ink pens around original documents.) Check out museum resources only after you've done some preliminary research from tertiary sources like books or magazines so as to know what you're looking for; that way you won't waste time--your own, or the museum curator's.

ART AND FOLK ART MUSEUMS may own paintings and drawings depicting the people and activities of the period that interests you. Remember that some works are allegorical; others are done long after an event--you find Biblical scenes enacted by people in Regency-period clothing. Formal portrait painters often worked within certain conventions (the face was the focal point; details of clothing were usually secondary.) Both they and folk artists sometimes painted the bodies at home, then added the faces of their patrons later, but other times they included fine detailing. Other folk artists were working for their own enjoyment and just drew what they saw. Some worked with wood, cloth or paper, giving you ideas for things to demonstrate. These museums may also have excellent libraries. Many mount excellent shows for which catalogs are available; some of these are quality books, full of facts and figures.

●◆ The NATIONAL ARCHIVES (WASHINGTON, DC 20408) are a wonderful source of information; it is truly our national library.

PUBLIC LIBRARIES generally have a good history section-- but don't limit yourself; art books, clothing, arms, and scientific books may tell you a great deal as well. You should be able to conduct genealogical research here, too.

STATE OR COUNTY HISTORICAL SOCIETY LIBRARIES, UNIVERSITY LIBRARIES. Although you may not be able to check out books here, you can often make photocopies. At an academic library, look at professional journals as well as at books; Some may only have circulations of 50 or less, but you may find a nugget of information that's appeared nowhere else.

Don't overlook the rare book room. Kansas City's Linda Hall Library, for instance, owns the entire set of original Diderot Encyclopedias containing information about hundreds of occupations . (There are numerous women pictured in unusual pursuits, by the way.)

If you find a specific person who interests you, contact your state's historical society library (or your subject's, if you've chosen someone out of state) for possible personal papers, letters, diaries, etc.

●◆  WILLS, PROBATES, CENSUS, AND MARRIAGE, BIRTH, AND DEATH RECORDS. Though less likely to reveal as much about women as men, you can still discover much about living conditions as well as specific people. Old cemeteries contain priceless tidbits in the information on their gravestones. Take photos as well as notes; it's easy to transpose numbers.

●◆  THE AMERICAN ANTIQUARIAN SOCIETY (185 Salisbury, Worcester, MA 01609-1634 ) has copies of perhaps 85% of all material printed before 1840--newspapers, broadsides, religious tracts, books. It's been around since the late 1790s.

The AMERICAN PHILOSOPHICAL SOCIETY (104 S. Fifth Street, Philadelphia, PA 19106-3386, 215-440-3400) was founded by Benjamin Franklin in the 1740s. This is also a fine source for period documents.

If you plan a visit, write or call both well ahead to make an appointment; they can take only a limited number of researchers a day.

●◆  BOOKS are among the best and most enjoyable resources. Most of the larger bookstores have a well-developed history, costume, art and science sections; check sale tables, as well. Bookstores that specialize in old or rare books may have volumes original to your time period--or published a lot closer to it than modern texts. Some are colored by the prevailing sensibilities of their time, if not the period they are about, but they can be a good place to start. Look especially for period encyclopedias, reference books and almanacs. These stores may also carry original documents; I have a two-page indenture that bequeaths land to a woman—unusual, but primary evidence that it did happen.

Look for books from reprint specialists like Dover Books, Readex Microprints, Burt Franklin, Zebrowski Historical Services and Publishing Company, King's Arms Press & Bindery, Heritage Books and others. See also University Microfilms' Directory of Dissertation Abstracts, which lists sources by author, subject and title. Many university presses also specialize in reprints. These are often exact replicas (except for the cover) of original volumes. Mail-order booksellers like Edward D. Hamilton and others often have closeouts on wonderful books.

•◊    As you read, don't overlook the author's BIBLIOGRAPHY for additional unusual or primary sources. Footnotes are good leads. Watch also for photo credits or captions. You may find an artifact owned by a museum you'll want to add to your vacation itinerary or discover a painting or primary source you can explore in more depth.

•◊    Several MAGAZINES are aimed at those interested in history, including *Smithsonian, Early American Life, American History Illustrated, American Heritage,* and *Muzzleloader,* usually in a library's database; general periodicals should be on disk. These offer usually well-researched pieces, photos or illustrations, and, often, complete bibliographies or resources. Look for picture credits as well.

•◊    If you are computer-literate, INTERNET or OTHER INFORMATIONAL SERVICES put you in touch with all the major museums in the nation, not to mention schools and universities worldwide. Join a discussion group on E-mail.

•◊    THE OFFICIAL DIRECTORY OF AMERICAN MUSEUMS ($150), available at libraries, is an annual publication of the American

Museum Association listing museums alphabetically by state, then within cities in each state.

**➡** **LIVING HISTORY AND GENEALOGICAL ORGANIZATIONS** often have newsletters, magazines or even books as part of their member resources. They include:

    ☞ **American Association of State and Local History,** 530 Church St., Nashville, TN 37219 615-255-2971

    ☞ **Association for Living Historical Farms and Agricultural Museums,** Conner Prairie, 13400 Allisonville Rd., Fishers, IN 46038

    ☞ **Brigade of the American Revolution;** Walter Myer, Adj., 27 Compton Ave., Plainfield, NJ 07063

    ☞ **Coalition of Historical Trekkers,** PO Box 1451, Andrews, TX 79714, 915-524-5119

    ☞ **Early American Industry Association,** 179 Mt. Pleasant Rd., Smithtown, NY 11787

    ☞ **Family History Library** (Mormon Church Genealogical Library), 705 W. Walnut, Independence, MO 64050

    ☞ **Living History Association,** PO Box 578, Wilmington, VT 05363

    ☞ **Living History Foundation,** c/o Peter Ryan, P.O. Box 220155, Chantilly, VA 22015, 703-955-HIST

    ☞ **Mid-west Open-air Museums Coordinating Council,** c/o Judith Sheridan, 8774 Rt. 45 NW, North Bloomfield, OH 44450

    ☞ **Society of Workers in Early Arts and Trades** (S.W.E.A.T.), 606 Lake Lena Blvd., Auburndale, FL 33823

## ➻SPECIALTY BOOK SOURCES:

BURT FRANKLIN (Lenox Hill Pub. & Dist. Co.), 235 E. 44th St. New York, NY 10017

DOVER PUBLICATIONS, INC. 180 Varick Street, NY, NY 10014

HERITAGE BOOKS, 1540 E. Pointer Ridge Place, Bowie, MD 20716

KING'S ARMS PRESS & BINDERY, PO Box 419, Oldwick, NJ 08858

READEX MICROPRINT CORPORATION, 58 Pine Street, New Canaan, CT 06840-5408 (800) 762-8182

UNIVERSITY MICROFILMS AND THE DIRECTORY OF DISSERTATION ABSTRACTS, Bell and Howell, 300 N. Zeeb Rd., Ann Arbor, MI 48106 (800) 521-0600

WILDE WEAVERY AND TRADING COMPANY, 602 E. 3rd St., Lee's Summit, MO 64063 (816) 524-7374

ZEBROWSKI HISTORICAL SERVICES AND PUBLISHING CO., RD 1, Box 53, Bloomingburg, NY 12721

## ➻ACCOUTREMENTS AND CLOTHING

Before ordering, do a bit of homework on what you actually *need*. Ask other reenactors what sutlers or suppliers they've found to be prompt and dependable. Make sure anyone you order from knows what you want, what your time period and persona might be, and all details of size, color, etc. of clothing ordered. You may want to ask around to find a local seamstress or tailor who is used to making period clothing, so you can be sure of personal fit.

Inclusion on this list in no way implies a guarantee of satisfaction. Policies and companies change or suspend operations, misunderstandings occur, and unforeseen circumstances arise. However, most of those listed have proven to the author to be good and dependable sources. Others were recommended by fellow reenactors.

Goose Bay Workshops
Peter and Debra Goebel
Rt. 1, Box 297C, Crozet, VA 22932; (703) 456-8717; Catalog $3.00; Fine copper and tinware as well as other accoutrements, including children's toys.

Wilde Weavery and Trading Company, Ed and C.J. Wilde
602 E. 3rd St., Lee's Summit, MO 64063 (816) 524-7374; Handwoven blankets, match coats, straps, sashes; haversacks, shooting bags, leatherwork, accoutrements, books; great attention to research, detail

51

**Tentsmiths**
Peter and Deborah Marques
Box 496, North Conway, NH
03860 (603) 447-2344; Catalog
$2.00; Fine tentage, well researched

**Bradley Company of the Fox**
Brian Bradley, Linda Marin
4330 N. State Rd. 110, Oshkosh,
WI 54904 (414) 233-5332
Catalog $3.00--Clothing (custom),
patterns, shoes, supplies, books

**Past Patterns**
Saundra Ros Altman
PO Box 7587, Grand Rapids, MI
49510; (616) 245-9456; Extremely
well-researched patterns with easy
to follow directions from 1812-1939

**Buffalo Enterprises**
308 W. King Street, Box 183, East
Berlin, PA 17316; (717) 259-9081
Catalog $4.00--Patterns, clothing,
supplies, antique eyewear

**Jas. Townsend & Son, Inc.**
133 N. First St., P.O. Box 415
Pierceton, IN 46562 (800) 338-
1665; Catalog $2.00--Patterns,
clothing, supplies, books--fast
service

**Textile Reproductions**
Kathleen B. Smith
Box 48, West Chesterfield,
MA 01084; (413) 296-4437;
Catalog $4.00; Wide range of

period fabrics, notions, kits, dyes

**Elegant Embellishments**
Beth and Chris Gilgun
29 Athol Rd., Warwick, MA 01378
(508) 544-3464--Greatcoats, capes,
jewelry, etc.

**Panther Primitives**
P.O. Box 32, Normantown, WV
25267 (304) 462-7718 --Catalog
$2.00--Books, patterns, clothing,
tents, supplies

**Amazon Drygoods**
2218 East 11th St., Davenport, IA
52803-3760 (319) 322-6800
General catalog, $3.00,,pattern
catalog $7.00--Shoe catalog $5.00;
Books, supplies, patterns, some
fabrics, clothing, period footwear

**G. Gedney Godwin, Inc.**
PO Box 100,Valley Forge, PA
19481 (610) 783-0670--Catalog
$4.95--Patterns, clothing, shoes,
supplies; military, medical, etc.

**Tidy's Storehouse**
1102 Hopewell Rd.; Oxford, PA
19330 (610) 932-8441; Period
patterns, clothing, supplies

**C&D Jarnagin Co.**
PO Box 1860; Corinth, MS 38834
(601) 287-4977--Catalog $3.00
Shoes, clothing, accoutrements

**Kannik's Korner**
Kathleen and Fritz Kannik
PO Box 1654
Springfield, OH 45501, (513) 325-8385--Books, well researched patterns, etc.

**The Farmer's Wife**; Jean M. Caruana; PO Box 664
Edgemont, PA 19028--Natural fabrics, threads, wools, etc.

**Smoke & Fire Co.**
PO Box 166, Grand Rapids, OH 43522 (419) 832-0303--Pottery, books, clothing, accoutrements

**Smiling Fox Forge**
3500 County Road 234, Fremont, OH 43420--(419) 334-8180; Catalog $5.00; blacksmith, childrens' goods, accoutrements

**James Burnley, "Mercer," and Mistress Trowbridge**
319 Oaktree Road, Williamsburg, VA 23188; (804) 253-1644; Ladies', mens', and children's shoes and a wonderful assortment of period fabrics and related items

**The Crowning Touch**
Libby Smith
1460 Autumn Knoll, Nashville, TN 37076-(615) 883-9501; Catalog $1.00; Ladies' caps, based on originals; patterns

**The Clothing Bureau**
PO Box 24492, Edina, MN 55424
(612) 823-2836; Museum-quality custom men's clothing, 1812, 1821, 1832 Military; some Civil War

**Historical Markers, Ltd.**
1221 S.E. 11th St., Lee's Summit, MO 64081--(816) 525-4826--Period fabrics, books, music

**Fiber Accents Handweavers**
Rob and Ardyth Stone
1007 Northwyck, Liberty, MO 64068 (816) 781-7017--17th, 18th, and 19th century handwoven blankets, etc., patterns, some books

**Threads of Time**
Lynn Symborski
327 Kenmore, Havertown, PA 19083; (215) 446-6356-(custom women's, some children's clothing; period dance.)

**Druid's Oak**
1654 New Windsor Ct.
Crofton, MD 21114; (410) 793-0309
Clothing for men and women

**Don Carpentier, Pottery**
Eastfield Village, Box 143, RD
East Nassau, NY 12062; (518) 766-2422; Wonderful mochaware, etc.; seminars at Eastfield Village on Early American Trades

**Rotten Randy and His Temple of Temptation**
Randy Simmermacher
125 Forrest Park Rd.
Bartlesville, OK 74003
(918) 337-0296; Good affordable copperware, a fine portable brazier

**Steve Wilson Journals**
5320 Northern
Raytown, MO 64133
(816) 358-9821
Two sizes, with 100% rag paper; leather-bound. Close with ties.

# ⚜BIBLIOGRAPHY⚜

Anderson, Jay; *A Living History Reader, Volume 1;* American Association for State and Local History, Nashville, TN; 1991.

_____; *A Living History Sourcebook;* American Association for State and Local History, Nashville, TN; 1985.

_____; *Time Machines; The World of Living History;* American Association of State and Local History, 1984.

Arnold, Janet; *Patterns of Fashion 1;* Drama Book Publishers, NY 1991.

Baumgarten, Linda; *Eighteenth Century Clothing at Williamsburg;* Colonial Williamsburg Foundation, VA; 1986.

Brackenridge, Henry Marie. *Early Western Travels,* Vol. 6, Reuben Gold Thwaites, editor; Arthur H. Clark Co., Cleveland, OH 1904.

Bradbury, John; *Travels in the Interior of America in the Years 1809, 1810, and 1811;* University of Nebraska Press, Lincoln, 1986.

Budd, Thomas; *Good Order Established in Pennsylvania and New Jersey, 1685;* Burt Franklin, NY 1971.

Carter II, Edward C., John C. Van Horne, and Chas. E. Brownell, Editors; *Latrobe's View of America, 1795-1820;* Yale U. Press, 1985.

Davidson, Marshall B.; *500 Years of Life in America; An Illustrated History;* Harry N. Abrams, Inc., NY 1983.

de Finiels, Nicolas; *An Account of Upper Louisiana;* edited by Carl J. Ekberg; University of Missouri Press, 1989.

Doddridge, Joseph; *The Settlement and Indian Wars of the Western Parts of Virginia and Pennsylvania, 1763-1783;* Heritage Books Inc., Bowie, Maryland, 1988.

Feduccia, Alan, editor; *Catesby's Birds of Colonial America*; University of North Carolina Press, Chapel Hill and London, 1985.
Ford, Alice, editor; *Audubon, By Himself; A Profile of John James Audubon*; Natural History Press, Garden City, NY 1969.

Fordham, Elias Pym; *Fordham's Personal Narrative, 1817-1818*; Heritage Books, Inc., Bowie, Maryland, 1989.

Gehret, Ellen J.; *Rural Pennsylvania Clothing*; George Shumway Publications, PA, 1976.

Grose, Captain Francis; *Classical Dictionary of the Vulgar Tongue*; edited by Eric Partridge, Dorset Press, NY 1992.

Hatt, Gudmund; *Memoirs of the American Anthropological Association*, Volume III, 1916; <occasions and Their Relation to Arctic Footwear; Kraus Reprint Corporation, NY 1964.

Hoffman, Ronald and Peter J. Albert, editors; *Women in the Age of the American Revolution*; U. Press of Virginia, Charlottesville, VA 1989.

Johnson, Cathy; *Living History; Drawing on the Past*; Graphics/Fine Arts Press, Excelsior Springs, MO, 1994.

Johnson, Susannah; *A Narrative of the Captivity of Mrs. Johnson (1757)*; Heritage Books, Inc., Bowie, MD; 1990.

Kannik, Kathleen; *The Lady's Guide to Plain Sewing; by a Lady*; Kannik's Korner, Springfield, OH, 1993.

Kauffman, Henry J.; , *Early American Copper, Tin and Brass*; Medill McBride Co.; NY; 1950 edition,

Knapke, Luke B., Editor, *Liwwat Boke, 1807-1882 Pioneer*, Minster Historical Society, Minster, OH 1987.

Knight, Sarah Kemble; *Journal of Madame Knight (1704)*; Applewood Books, 1992.

Kyoto Costume Institute; *Revolution in Fashion, 1715-1815;* Several contributing authors, including Janet Arnold; Abbeville Press, NY 1990.

Lederer, Jr.,Richard M.; *Colonial American English;* Verbatim, Essex, Connecticut, 1985.

March, David D., Ph.D.; *History of Missouri,;* Lewis Historical Publishing Co., NY 1967.

Martin, J.P.; *Private Yankee Doodle;* edited by George E. Scheer; Eastern Acorn Press, 1993.

McKnight, Charles; *Our Western Border 100 Years Ago,* J.C. McCurdy and Co., Cincinnnati, Chicago, and St. Louis, 1876.

Montgomery, Florence M.; *Textiles in America, 1650-1870;* W. W. Norton & Co.; NY, 1984.

Pitot, James; *Observations on the Colony of Louisiana from 1796 to 1802;* Louisiana State University Press, Baton Rouge, 1979.

Prucha, Paul Francis; *Handbook for Research in American History;* University of Nebraska Press, Lincoln; 1987.

Pyne, W. H.; *Pyne's British Costumes;* Wordsworth Editions, Ltd., Herfordshire, Great Britain, 1989.

_____; *Rustic Vignettes for Artists and Craftsmen;* Dover Publications, NY 1977; a collection of 641 engravings from Ackermann's Edition of the "Microcosm".

Quennell, Peter; *Hogarth's Progress;* Viking Press, NY 1955.
Robin, C.C.; *Voyage to Louisiana (1803-1805)* Pelican Publishing Co., New Orleans; 1966.

Rumford, Beatrix and Carolyn Weekley; *Treasures of American Folk Art from the Abby Aldrich Rockefeller Folk Art Center;* Colonial Williamsburg Foundation, Bulfinch Press, Boston, 1989.

Schultz, Christian; *Travels on an Inland Voyage in 1807-1808;* Gregg Press, Ridgewood, NJ 1968.

Shelley, Donald A. introduction; *Lewis Miller Sketches and Chronicles;* The Historical Society of York Co., York, PA, 1966; reproductions of Miller's journal pages.

Stoddard, Amos; *Sketches, Historical and Descriptive, of Louisiana (1812);* AMS Press, Inc., NY 1973.

Waugh, Norah; *Cut of Men's Clothes, 1600-1930;* Theatre Arts Books, NY 1964.
_____; Cut of Women's Clothes, 1600-1930; Theatre Arts Book, NY 1968.

Woodmason, Charles; *The Carolina Backcountry on the Eve of the Revolution;* Richard J. Hooker, Ed.; University of North Carolina Press; Chapel Hill; 1953.

Wright, Merideth; *Everyday Dress of Rural America, 1783-1800;* Dover Publications, NY 1992.

Marshes Station
Tennessee

# ❧GET TO KNOW YOUR PERSONA❧

       Fill out this quick form, if you like, to fix in your mind the details of your chosen persona. Put yourself in his or her place. Have fun.


Name_____Birthday_____

Place of Birth, Nationality_____

Economic Status_____

Interests, skills_____

Education (Where? Why? How?)_____

Parents' names, place of birth_____

Brothers, sisters?_____

Married, children?_____

How do you make your living?_____

Why do you live where you do?_____

Health status?_____

Etc. (any notes on character or interests you want to include)_____

_____

_____

_____

_____

Notes:

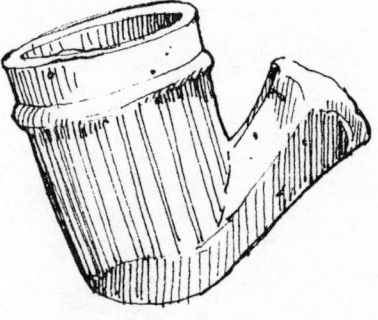

**Notes:**

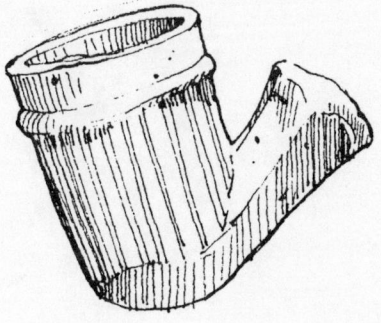

*Upcoming Books in this series from*

# *Graphics/Fine Arts Press:*

*A Life of One's Own: Independent Women of America's Past*

*Common Clothing--1730-1850*

*A Trekker's Guide to Useful Wild Plants*

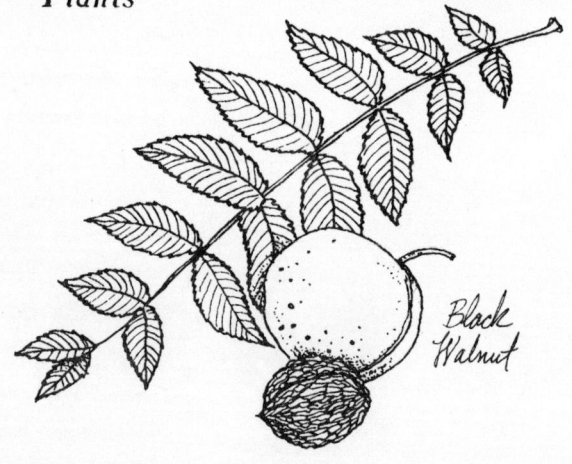

Black Walnut